A LIFE WORTH LIVING

"I consider myself to have been incredibly blessed by the grace of Christ in so many ways, none greater than to have come under the influence of Chuck Reinhold at a formative stage in my life. I've had many wonderful mentors over a lifetime of ministry but none to rival Chuck. His enthusiasm for Christ and laser focus, his humor and motivational gifts, his friendship and guidance, have all contributed mightily to what I've had to offer others in the Lord over a lifetime in ministry. My wish is that this book would find its way into the hands of many others who desire to be used by Christ, that they too might benefit as I have."

—**Dr. David "Tuck" Knupp**,
Young Life staff/Presbyterian minister

"In this book we are confronted by stories that transmit the love that Chuck has poured into the lives of so many to encourage, equip, and enable them to serve Jesus. These stories and principles will challenge and motivate the reader to do likewise."

—**William Malarkey**, Professor Emeritus of Internal Medicine
at the Ohio State University Wexner Medical Center

"I first met Chuck Reinhold when I was a new follower of Jesus, as he and Linda took me in and discipled me around their kitchen table. If there is one word to describe Chuck, it would be 'encourager.' He always gives of himself—just like Jesus. *A Life Worth Living* captures so well the impact Chuck has had on so many lives, including my own. Reading it will inspire and challenge you. It is a reflection of Chuck's heart—a true testimony of Hebrews 12:1–3. He has faithfully run the race with endurance, keeping his eyes fixed on Jesus, impacting countless people of all ages, walks of life, and circumstances."

—**Jim Harrelson**, Vice President,
Samaritan's Purse/Operation Christmas Child

"Running a football behind Pitt blocker Mike Ditka. Ending the life of a hissing Ethiopian adder. Not offending Boris, the caviar-toting KGB agent. Such adventures pale in comparison to Chuck Reinhold's greatest calling—to befriend teenagers. Thousands of us.

"An intriguing speaker, Chuck managed to bridge the distance of age with high school campers. Fun and ever-smiling, he took the brunt of Young Life skits and singalongs. He seemed to know me, to know all of us, and to care about our best futures.

"Our twenty-first century is desperate to find joy. To laugh again. The Lord knows this, and He's given us Chuck Reinhold, a pure and passionate channel to point us to Jesus Christ, the source of love and joy.

"In these beautiful pages, we find a quality of kindness worth studying. Kindness that draws from its source. Kindness that tells the truth. Kindness that saves and changes lives. The summer of 1975, at Young Life's Saranac Village in the Adirondack Mountains of New York, one of those lives was mine. I am forever grateful."

—**Kelly Monroe Kullberg**, Founder, The Veritas Forum,
Author, *Finding God Beyond Harvard*, Young Life volunteer

"Last year, at Young Life's Global Leadership Conference, I was in a room with several African staff. One night, many of them were in the dorm lobby 'facetiming' their families. I was talking with one of them and found out he was from Ethiopia. I told him my Young Life leader was Chuck Reinhold and that he had helped start Young Life in Ethiopia. The man next to him, who was not from Ethiopia, held up his hands dramatically and said, 'Oh no, Chuck Reinhold is the father of Young Life in *all* of Africa!'"

—**Joe Marks**, Young Life staff

"Met Chuck thirty-five years ago when my eldest of three sons joined Young Life. Fairly quickly, we parents got involved with YL and started holding meetings at our home. A great friendship developed. He was and continues to be a passionate, consistently enthusiastic 'warrior' for Christ with a humble persona and sense of humor that is contagious. His style of developing personal relationships with kids is incredibly effective. It ought to be the technique all churches use, not just Young Life.

"Since I would put myself in the sheepdog category, Chuck's appeal is as a manly man who brings his strong manhood to the portrayal of Christ as a powerful, yet compassionate and forgiving Son of God. Chuck always walks the talk. With Chuck, it is never about him, it is about Him or about you. If you are becoming a Christian, growing in the faith, teaching, or leading in any walk of life, this is a worthy read about servant leadership."

—**Woody Johnson**, Retired Special Agent in Charge, FBI,
Former Commander, National Hostage Rescue Team

"Chuck Reinhold made me a disciple of Jesus. You will understand as you read *A Life Worth Living* that Chuck's mission was and is to make this true for people wherever he met them. He wanted Jesus to make my life worth living.

"One of the wonderous ways he did that with me was the art of the personal question: 'Mike, how long do you expect to be a Christian?' It was a question that defied a quick answer and a question that has echoed in me for a lifetime. I answer the question Chuck asked me every day, 'Lord, I'm planning for the long haul.'"

—**Mike O'Leary**, President, Young Life of Canada

"Shortly after I graduated from high school, I met Chuck and Linda, together with Doug Holladay, in Ethiopia. Little did I know that meeting them would profoundly impact my life. I will never forget their sincere love for people, their desire and passion for young people to know God, their generosity, and their humor. I will never forget Chuck's short, impactful message of the Gospels, his prayers and encouragement, and Linda's beautiful welcoming smile and her sweet, caring spirit.

"After many years of absence from my home country, I returned to Ethiopia and, in 1997, together with Chuck and Linda, we launched Young Life in Addis Ababa's poor neighborhood called Kore. As a result, many have found faith in Christ and their lives profoundly transformed.

"Today, not only is Young Life impacting kids' lives in Ethiopia but also throughout other countries in Africa. I thank God for bringing Chuck and Linda into my life at such a young age. I have benefited from their love, fellowship, and prayers for the past forty-seven years of my life. I have no doubt many who read this book, particularly those with the heart of ministering to kids, will find this book inspiring and be blessed by Chuck's selfless, single-minded service to his Lord."

—**Abraham Fiseha**, Co-founder of Youth
Impact Ethiopia, Addis Ababa, Ethiopia

A LIFE
WORTH
LIVING

What I Learned
Along the Way

CHUCK REINHOLD

NASHVILLE

NEW YORK • LONDON • MELBOURNE • VANCOUVER

A LIFE WORTH LIVING
What I Learned Along the Way

© 2019 **CHUCK REINHOLD**

Published in New York, New York, by Morgan James Publishing. Morgan James is a trademark of Morgan James, LLC. www.MorganJamesPublishing.com

The Morgan James Speakers Group can bring authors to your live event. For more information or to book an event visit The Morgan James Speakers Group at www.TheMorganJamesSpeakersGroup.com.

All Scripture quotations, unless otherwise indicated, are taken from The Holy Bible, New International Version®, NIV®. Copyright © 1973, 1978, 1984, 2011 by Biblica, Inc.® Used by permission. All rights reserved worldwide.

ISBN 978-1-64279-129-7 paperback
ISBN 978-1-64279-130-3 eBook
ISBN 978-1-64279-131-0 hardcover
Library of Congress Control Number: 2018947654

Editor
Jeff Chesemore

Cover Design by:
Rachel Lopez
www.r2cdesign.com

Interior Design by:
Bonnie Bushman
The Whole Caboodle Graphic Design

In an effort to support local communities, raise awareness and funds, Morgan James Publishing donates a percentage of all book sales for the life of each book to Habitat for Humanity Peninsula and Greater Williamsburg.

Get involved today! Visit
www.MorganJamesBuilds.com

Chuck with Linda, the love of his life!

To my wonderful wife, Linda, the love of my life!

I married the most wonderful person in the world and never have I doubted it. I give Linda credit for any success I've had in my life (except football, of course!) because she has always been such an encouragement and support in everything I've done. She's given me lots of love and forgiveness and she's been my advisor and best friend. She has blessed me in so many ways. I don't think anything in this book would have happened without her influence on my life for over fifty years. We have been through so many wonderful adventures in our life together, and I'm thankful every day to the Lord for His guidance, direction, and many blessings.

TABLE OF CONTENTS

Like Writing on Water   *xiii*

Foreword   *xvii*

Where Everything Begins and Ends   *xxi*

A Young Life Glossary of Terms   *xxiv*

Chapter 1	A Proper Introduction	1
Chapter 2	Every Morning	9
Chapter 3	Living the Wild Life	16
Chapter 4	A Lifelong Pioneer	24
Chapter 5	"The" City	33
Chapter 6	Transition, Tragedy, and Training	44
Chapter 7	The Training Program Document	51
Chapter 8	Working with "Big Kids"	58
Chapter 9	Back in the Saddle Again	71
Chapter 10	A Principled Man	87

Chapter 11   Ethiopia: The Sequel   91
Chapter 12   A New Vision   108

Afterword   *125*
Appendix   *128*
Chuck's Core Principles   *128*
Even More (!) Principles Learned Along the Way…   *130*
Bible Studies: Jesus and His Worship Time, Mark 1:35–38   *134*
Bible Studies: The Centurion's Servant, Luke 7:1–10   *137*
Recommended Books and Websites   *141*
Acknowledgements   *144*
About the Author   *147*

LIKE WRITING ON WATER

By Hollie Reinhold Birckhead and Josh Reinhold, Chuck's children

Dear Friends,

Our dad has had on his heart for years to write this book, but he hasn't been able to because of memory/dementia issues that have developed over the past fifteen years or so—issues believed to be the result of injuries suffered while he was playing football in high school and college more than fifty years ago. As his children, we felt God called us to help put this book together. (The Acknowledgements section of this book is long for good reason. There have been so many people who have contributed!)

When our dad first noticed he was starting to lose his memory, he would say it's "like writing on water." He would remember things for a short time and then they would disappear, just like when you throw a stone in a pond and the ripples start strong but then quickly fade away.

We want to begin this book by sharing this treasured letter our dad wrote years ago, as it speaks to his mindset at the time he first realized his memory was fading. This letter also speaks to his heart, his love for the Lord, and his deep desire to share Christ so we may all know Him deeply ourselves.

January 2, 2004

Dear Friends:

I have much to be thankful for. You all have been great in your prayers and support for me. I don't have the same energy. I am as alert as I ever was in the moment of conversation and thought, but it is difficult to recall facts from yesterday or even an hour ago.

[What I'm] learning is that I have been spoiled with what God has given me at birth and the friends, education, and experiences along the way that have helped me to compete well in this world. I don't think I took it for granted, but I have an opportunity now to accept myself as I am. I realize that I don't have the same capacity I had and can't compete at the same level.

I have a handicap and I want to be thankful in it and trust the Lord to give me ways to trust and serve Him in the midst of it. Already I feel a compassion in me for people at a new level. I look for ways to serve people in the little things that were missing in my life. I am finding value in the little things I took for granted. I need people to help me where I did not before. I am humbled at the new awareness of how much and unselfishly Linda has served me all of these years with such a Christ-like attitude. She does it without a hint of making me think I am weak in any way. It is a new area for me in knowing the Lord and trusting Him and depending on others in new ways. I must depend on others in areas that in the past I took pride in. It is a new world for me, and I think it is enhancing my relationship with the Lord and others. My prayer is it will actually broaden and deepen my capacity to serve and not limit it.

Please pray for me that I will learn everything the Lord wants me to in this next phase of my life. Thanks for going into this new year with me.

By the way, read Luke 5:1–11. It is a wonderful and inspiring passage to send us into the new year. It is about the fishermen fishing all night and catching nothing (not a good feeling). Jesus sends them out again and they catch more fish than they could have dreamed of. The fishing nets were breaking (nets made for fish). The fishing boats sinking because of too many fish (boats made to carry fish). Now, how many fish did they have in the beginning and how many did they have in the end? I might have tricked you into saying "zero fish in the beginning and multitudes in the end." You would be wrong again. There were zero fish in the beginning and zero fish at the end. They left them all on the shore and followed Jesus.

What was the point? It is all about Jesus. They needed the fish before but now that they have this TRUER picture of Jesus and His love and power, they just wanted Him plus nothing. Remember that on the boat Peter responded to Jesus when he saw all of those fish by saying "Depart from me for I am a sinful man." (KJV) Jesus did not bring it up. Peter's sin was not the issue for Jesus on whether He gave him fish or not. Jesus loved those fishermen in ways that they could understand. Lots and lots of fish. But he gave it to them when they were sinful men and they knew it. Jesus' love changes us as sinners. He loves us first. That is what we do in Young Life.

But the point I would like for us to consider for this new year is to count our blessings (the catch of fish) from the past year. Let's be thankful, love what God has done for us, and leave it on the shore of the past year. Leave our "fish" in 2003 and let us walk off with Jesus. Let's make our goals knowing that we are going through the year with Him, not for Him. He is going to be with us and lead us and provide what is needed. Can you doubt Jesus if you were Peter?

That is what I want to do. I want to go back to Ethiopia with Linda and see everything as new. I want to get off the plane with Jesus knowing that He can do it all and in abundance if needed. But He is the One. Can you imagine going into this new year with just hopes and dreams, but without Christ? Our privilege is to know that our one purpose is to help kids know that Jesus Christ loves them, died for them, and will go through the rest of their lives with Him.

Love,
Chuck (alongside my beloved wife, Linda)

Chuck and Linda's kids: Josh, Hollie, and Chuckie in May 2007.

FOREWORD

Joni Eareckson Tada

Before You Begin...

Of all the people who've been blessed under Chuck Reinhold's watch, how did I land this honor? I could name twenty friends—just from Woodlawn High School—who'd give anything to fill this page with reflections about him. But I guess I'm it. And I hope I do the rest of you proud as I remember Chuck and what he means to us all.

Because there's just something about the man. And that something is Jesus.

"If Jesus were around today, he'd be *that* guy," I said to my teammates, nodding at the man on the sidelines. The very cool guy not only knew my name, he cheered all us lowly sophomores on through the entire first half. Even the older girls on varsity. He seemed to know everybody, even the coaches. So why would he be so nice to a bunch of kids on JV?

Not like a dad, but more like the encouraging older brother you never had. He seemed so engaging, in a winsome, genuine way... as though he were really interested in *you*. *Yep, Jesus would be like that,* I reflected later in the locker room.

Before long, the varsity girls asked a few of us to come to Young Life club. "We can't explain Young Life," they said, "You have to experience it to understand it!" We fell for the bait, and the following Wednesday night, we tumbled into the meeting hall, ready for fun. Up front was the leader, the same cool guy still relating to kids as though he'd known them for years. "That's Chuck Reinhold," a senior girl explained. I stared for a minute. *Wow. And to think... he knows my name.*

Young people who sat under Chuck's leadership never quite got over that. He *liked* us. He called us by name. And when he would stand before 200 club kids with his J.B. Phillips Bible in hand, Chuck made you believe that God liked you, too. And was calling *you* by name. His command of Scripture was that good, and his winning way of presenting Jesus' message made the Bible come alive. Sure, everyone liked being with Chuck... but we *really* liked being with his Savior.

Maybe the apostle Paul told others to, "Follow my example as I follow the example of Christ himself." But Chuck could say the same. It's how people respond when humility and a pure heart are so evident in a man. Whether a student or an adult, you learned by his example to take prayer seriously, love God's Word deeply, and delight in telling others about Christ.

I remember the summer of 1966, sitting with him up on Cheyenne Mountain that rose majestically behind Young Life's Star Ranch camp in Colorado. A few campers and I had raced Chuck up the rugged dirt path to Alpine Point. Catching my breath, I found a seat on a rock next to him. We were awed by the breathtaking vista. The air was pine-crisp, and I felt as though I were sitting on top of the world.

All was silent. Then my club leader turned and said, "Joni, you know you can really do something big for God, don't you?" He liked doing that—casting large visions for young people, especially when they lacked vision for themselves. But the way I figured it, if Chuck believed it… I believed it. Later, back in my cabin, I reflected on his words. What big things could God possibly do with me?

Less than a year later, I found out. I broke my neck right after high school graduation. It wasn't the "something big" I was expecting, to say the least. Quadriplegia was a game-changer. Chuck came several times to the hospital to visit, even after they transferred me across town to rehab. He stood above me, tightly hugging the guard rail of my bed. This was not Young Life. This was not fun. But after a little light conversation, he said softly, "I'd like to ask God to heal you." It was a reasonable thing to pray. None of us knew if this quadriplegia would be permanent.

"You can pray," I told him. "But I think I've got some lessons to learn before I walk again." It was an unusually wise thing for a kid to say. But looking into the piercing eyes of Chuck Reinhold, I could not do anything less than be honest.

Fifty years have passed since that poignant encounter—Chuck went on to Rochester, New York, and married Linda, one of the wonderful seniors who first invited me to the club. I went on to learn a lot of those lessons God wanted to teach me. The best lesson? There *are* more important things in life than walking. It's a lesson I pass on to thousands of people with disabilities through a global ministry called Joni and Friends. Chuck was right. I guess I ended up doing something big for God—or more accurately, He did something big through me.

More than fifteen years ago, when my husband Ken and I were working among people with disabilities in Ethiopia, we stopped by Chuck and Linda's home in Addis Ababa—at that point, Chuck was taking Young Life global, even into some of the darkest parts of the world. That evening happened to be club night, and the Reinhold's house quickly filled up with Ethiopian high schoolers. When Chuck got up to start things, I felt as though I were transported decades back to Woodlawn's Wednesday night club—he was still the same cool guy relating to kids as though he'd known them for years, calling each by name. He was still presenting Jesus' message in a way that made the Bible come alive.

Chuck Reinhold is a man of great influence, and it's impossible to overstate the legacy he has built into tens of thousands of lives. He has helped shape and maintain the distinctives of Young Life more than any other leader, except for a few others, like Jim Rayburn, founder of Young Life. Chuck is a rare breed, so take time to get to know the man on these pages… and if you already know him, then learn more of his story.

Never will you meet a more large-hearted brother in Christ. And I just bet when he sees you in heaven… he'll call you out of the crowd by your name.

Joni Eareckson Tada
Joni and Friends International Disability Center

WHERE EVERYTHING
BEGINS AND ENDS

"I want to be an enthusiastic lover of Christ and desire to cultivate a relationship with Him in every situation."

A little about Chuck...

Charles Emerson Reinhold was born in 1939. Chuck Reinhold was re-born in 1957. With Chuck, everything begins and ends with Jesus.

Now seventy-nine and struggling with short-term memory issues, Chuck has spent his entire adult life in the service of his beloved Savior, primarily through the ministry of Young Life, a mission devoted to "introducing adolescents to Jesus Christ and helping them grow in their faith." It may sound like hyperbole to say Chuck is one of the most influential people in Young Life's history but today generations of men and women can point to him as their spiritual father (or grandfather) in the faith.

Consider this remembrance from longtime Young Life staff, Rick Rogan:

"In September of 2016, I sat in a meeting with a dozen other Young Life staff. About a handful of us are on staff and still on staff because of Chuck. Each day over our time together, someone in that room quoted what they learned from Chuck over twenty-five years ago. 'There is nothing more important than your personal walk with Jesus Christ.' 'There are no shortcuts to spiritual leadership.' 'The Muslims don't even think their bible is the Word of God and they memorized it, what about you?' 'I am glad that Young Life didn't stop before they reached my high school.' 'People are more important than programs.'

"There is more because there is more to Chuck. Actually, I take that back! There is not more to Chuck. There is just one thing to Chuck, and that one thing is a person—Jesus Christ."

Stories like this can be multiplied throughout the mission. Countless Young Life staff and volunteers have this man to thank for the rich wisdom, counsel, and training they've received during their time under his leadership.

Chuck's influence doesn't stop here, though. He's been a powerful presence in whatever church he's been a part of—whether by attending, volunteering, or serving on staff. His is a Kingdom voice.

What's in a Name?

The surname *Reinhold* is Germanic and at its most basic, means "wise ruler." Other variations can render its meaning to "ruler's advisor." Both are apt descriptions of Chuck.

This "wise ruler's" leadership principles—sometimes borrowed, sometimes his own—have traveled around the world with the men and women who put them into practice as they minister to others.

As for playing the part of "ruler's advisor," Chuck's had the ear of countless leaders in authority over him. His humble encouragements, reminders, and admonitions have helped guide ministry presidents, pastors, and others needing a timely word from the Lord.

Chuck would be the first to point out, however, that he has not "arrived" but is still in the process of becoming like Jesus. His goal in writing this book is not to proclaim his own greatness or glorify his own accomplishments but to direct others to his First Love.

The Principle of the Thing

In each chapter we'll look at principles Chuck embraces; he's gleaned these insights from the Scriptures, prayer, friends, seminars/conferences, reading great books, and various other sources. Throughout his life he's written these insights down on the back of envelopes, note cards, napkins, in margin notes, etc. Why include these? Because Chuck wouldn't want a book about him that didn't include specific ways to encourage others in Christ!

Principles Learned Along the Way...

- We need to cultivate our relationship with Christ in every situation. (Col. 3:11, J.B. Phillips New Testament: "Christ is all that matters.")
- Obedience is the key to experiencing Jesus Christ. (John 14:21)
- Live for Christ when no one is around. (Col. 3:23–24)

"The most excellent method he had found of going to God was that of doing our common business without any view of pleasing men, and (as far as we are capable) purely for the love of God." *The Practice of the Presence of God*, Brother Lawrence

(Can't get enough of principles like these? There's even more in the Appendix!)

A YOUNG LIFE
GLOSSARY OF TERMS

Chuck Reinhold has a long tenure with Young Life, an organization whose mission is *introducing adolescents to Jesus Christ and helping them grow in their faith.* Like most organizations, Young Life has a culture and terminology all its own. Here's a quick guide to some of these frequently used terms.

area director. A Young Life staff person who gives direction to the staff, volunteers, and ministries under their supervision. (Areas most often encompass a county or township.)

assignment. A summer session at one of Young Life's camps where staff members and their families serve in various capacities, from speaking to program to leading volunteer work crew and summer staff.

Campaigners. A weekly gathering for kids who want to go deeper in their faith, capitalized because the word derives from the Young Life Campaign, the original mission name.

camp. Resort-quality properties where kids have the best week of their lives while experiencing the Gospel.

club. A party with a purpose to gather kids for fun and a simple message on God's love for them.

incarnational (ministry). The essence of Young Life's approach to ministry, modeled by Jesus Christ, who "became flesh and blood and moved into the neighborhood." (John 1:14, *The Message* paraphrase)

leadership meetings. Regular gatherings of staff and volunteer leaders for the purpose of fellowship and ministry training.

program. The umbrella term for the combination of mixers, skits, games, and humor at clubs and camps that, together, captivate the most disinterested and "furthest-out" kids, and everyone in between.

regional director. A Young Life staffer who gives direction to the area directors and other staff under their supervision. (Each region is made up of several areas.)

Say-So. The opportunity for kids to declare they have made a decision to follow Jesus Christ. See Psalm 107:2 (KJV), "Let the redeemed of the Lord say so."

summer staff. A volunteer experience at camp for college students or who are college- or post-college-age, in positions requiring maturity and a strong, non-verbal witness.

volunteers. The lifeblood of Young Life—adults who work in direct ministry with kids or on the area committee.

work crew. A volunteer experience at camp for high school students that deepens faith through service and community.

Young Life camps mentioned in this book:

- **Frontier Ranch**, Buena Vista, Colorado
- **Lake Champion**, Glen Spey, New York
- **Rockbridge Alum Springs**, Lexington, Virginia
- **Saranac Village**, Saranac Lake, New York
- **Southwind**, Ocklawaha, Florida
- **Star Ranch**, Colorado Springs, Colorado (1946–1972)
- **Trail West Lodge**, Buena Vista, Colorado
- **Windy Gap**, Weaverville, North Carolina

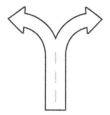

Chapter 1

A PROPER INTRODUCTION

"I'm glad Young Life didn't stop before it came to my high school."

I f there's one quote the larger mission of Young Life associates with Chuck, it's this one. Perhaps it's so memorable because it's both personal and universal...

Honestly, how many of us have thought the exact same thing? How many of us have thanked God that Young Life didn't stop before it found us?

Well, "Young Life" is really a friend. And for Chuck, that friend was Bob Scott.

As He always does, God brought Bob into Chuck's life at just the right time. As a high school junior, Chuck was ready for the great adventure of following Jesus (even if he didn't know it!). Up until that point, however, Chuck had concerned himself with other things…

Athletics and Atheism

My childhood was a foreshadowing of what my adult life would also be—a series of transitions. My family's eastward moves—from Stillwater, Oklahoma, to Akron, Ohio, to Pittsburgh, Pennsylvania—were all born out of my father's fluid job status. I was crazy about my parents and my older brother, Dick, and younger sister, Gwin.

Dick was two years older and a tough kid and he made *me* a tough kid! Gwin was eight years younger, and I've always been sad I didn't grow up with her.

In my early years, I fell in love with sports and quickly flourished. Once we arrived in Pittsburgh's run-down West End, I discovered other things, too. Dick and I roamed the rough streets, where we learned to fight and steal; a favorite pastime was snatching candy from the local store. If our family had stayed, I believe I would have ended up in prison. Fortunately, my father found a well-paying job in Mt. Lebanon, a middle-class suburb southwest of the city, where we moved in the early 1950s when I was in middle school. It would prove to be a turning point in my life.

No matter what else I dabbled in, sports were my primary obsession. Our home sat "a stone's throw away" from the high school—on a hill overlooking the sports fields—where I would soon letter in football, basketball, baseball, and track.

During these heady days, sports became my religion. Despite my family's faithful attendance at the local Episcopal church, I regarded myself as an atheist. Even though I was paid to sing in the choir and serve as an acolyte, I really saw church as a perfect opportunity to be a cut up!

At that time, I wasn't interested in anything "churchy." I thought Christianity was for those who didn't know how to have fun!

Why?

When you're a junior on the football team and the senior captain invites you somewhere, odds are you'll go. That's why it didn't take me long to say "yes" when Fritz Walker invited me to Young Life club.

I didn't even ask what Young Life was about. I happily went, because Fritz invited me to go. It sounded exciting and adventurous.

When I entered the house that spring night in 1956, I was awestruck. I couldn't believe how friendly everyone was and how happy they were to see me.

"Why?" I wondered...

I quickly settled in and especially enjoyed singing the songs. Energetic at first, then slowing down before the message, the music made an impression; all in all, quite a memorable evening.

The Time of My Life

Soon, Fritz Walker came calling again. Would I go on a Young Life weekend?

Packed in a room at the Bedford Springs Hotel with four other guys, I wasn't too impressed by the accommodations. As I remember, there wasn't much to do, but I still had the time of my life. I didn't even make the first club meeting. My friend and I snuck into the rooms of some guys from another school and short-sheeted their beds. (We were so clever.)

Later that night, when the leaders and kids gathered in small groups to discuss the day, I learned that I'd missed some wonderful singing and a talk on one of the miracles Jesus performed.

It sounded interesting, but I was still indifferent. In less than twenty-four hours, all this was about to change.

Going 0 for 10

The talk in club the next morning was on the Ten Commandments; nothing seemingly revolutionary about that. I obviously had heard of them, but so what?

As the speaker explained the spirit behind each commandment (e.g., "thou shalt not commit murder" didn't have to be actual murder; hatred was enough to break the commandment), he asked us to grade ourselves on each one.

I was zero for ten. You'd think I wouldn't care, but it was just the opposite. For the first time in my life, I realized I was a complete and total sinner.

This self-proclaimed atheist was devastated.

The talk made me realize there *was* a God and I was in bad shape. I was lost and knew my sin condemned me and separated me from God and heaven. I knew I was missing out on something really wonderful.

I spent the afternoon playing sports—not with the same joy, but probably winning (that's a joke... maybe.) I look back on that morning and thank the Lord. I was prepared for His truth.

A New Adventure

That night I sat on the floor transfixed by the speaker's verse-by-verse description of Jesus' crucifixion (also known as the "cross talk").

Every now and then, the speaker would pause and say, "He was doing this for you and me." It was so powerful, and God in His love was speaking personally to me.

The desperate lows of that morning had been overshadowed by this new development.

I was still reeling from the sin talk and feeling totally guilty and unworthy of the Lord. Then I learned God loved me and His Son died on the cross for MY sins. It was the greatest truth I had ever heard!

In mere hours, the point of all this new information would become clear.

On Sunday morning, the speaker explained that the cross now enabled anyone to receive Jesus' invitation to a new life with him.

I couldn't believe it! I left that meeting full of a joy I'd never experienced. I immediately went to my leader, Bob Scott, and asked him what I had to do to receive God's love and forgiveness. He explained all I had to do was receive Him into my life as my Lord and Savior. He opened the Bible to Rev. 3:20, which has continued to be one of my favorite verses. "Behold, I stand at the door and knock. If anyone hears my voice and opens the door, I will come in and eat with him and him with me." (KJV) What a marvelous promise of God to people who have no hope of ever earning it!

I prayed and asked Jesus into my life. I felt the change immediately.

This continues to be the greatest moment of my life (and I've had many since). I was beginning a new adventure with the wonderful, loving God of the universe.

I wasn't alone in my delight—my friends celebrated right along with me. Unbeknownst to me, so many of the Campaigner kids had been praying for me.

My lifelong friend Carl Templin recalls, "Chuck stood up at the weekend and thrilled everyone who had been praying for him by stating he had given his life to Jesus Christ. (That was, of course, after he and his Mount Lebanon teammates had virtually destroyed the hotel. Poor Bob Scott!)"

Sue Smith, a friend since middle school said, "We'd have Young Life club at my house and Chuck's whole entourage of guys would come, so then everyone would. I remember when the word got out that Chuck was going to camp at Bedford Springs, many of us prayed and prayed he would meet the Lord. To have him become a Christian and channel his gifts to honor Christ, we knew could be huge for our school and the Kingdom."

Mercy One Morning

I took to my new life in Christ as naturally as I did with sports; but just like the hours spent on the gridiron, track or hardwood, I'd need proper coaching.

Bob Scott continued to live out the calling of every Young Life leader by pointing me to Jesus, both verbally and non-verbally. He became my "spiritual" father, pouring his life into his young friend.

Despite living an hour away, Bob drove into town once a week to meet with me in the morning before school.

I know it was a big sacrifice for him, but I would have never known by how he acted or what he said. He was always happy to see me, and he let me know it by what he said, his smile, and his actions.

One morning I ran out the door pacing myself to walk into homeroom just as the late bell rang—I had it down to a science. As I came out the door, though, I saw Bob, who'd been waiting for me in his car for an hour. I had completely forgotten about the scheduled meeting. Bob met me with a smile and drove me the short distance to school.

This moment could have been one of humiliation and defeat, but because Bob handled it so gracefully, it became one of life's teachable moments for me.

Bob never brought that incident up again. For sure it was not a wasted effort on his part. I think it taught me more about God's faithfulness and love due to Bob's kind response than if I remembered and met with him on time. Bob completely forgave me.

I am and will be forever grateful for that memory of love when so undeserved. I owe Bob so much because he gave me everything worth having—Jesus.

"The Best Medicine"

Over his seventy-nine years, Chuck has remained gregarious and full of life. Chuck's humor, *whether a gift to others or self-inflicted*, has endeared the man to so many over the years. Throughout the book, we'll enjoy "snapshots" of the lighter side of Chuck. Here's the first…

PURE CHUCK (circa 1970s)

"Chuck used his two false front teeth to good effect. (He lost his teeth in junior high when he was racing with friends, looked behind him to see how they were doing, turned back around, and ran into a post.)

"In the middle of a conversation with you he might just casually let them drop and then pop them right back up—always worth a laugh. On the weekend camp he did 'the movie skit' (I still think he was the absolute best I ever saw at it) and filled his mouth with gum, popcorn, and soda and had gotten beat up for about the third time as was the custom of the script. The crowd was in stitches and the skit was over when Chuck realized that his false teeth were gone. They had to be somewhere in that big ball of gum and popcorn. They had to retrieve the ball (already thrown in the trash) and pull through it until they found his teeth."

—Tuck Knupp, longtime Young Life staff

Principles Learned Along the Way…

- People don't have a problem with Jesus Christ—they have a problem with their *introduction* to Jesus Christ—because a wrong introduction leads to a wrong conclusion every time.

- Music is a big part of our gospel proclamation. The songs in club had a wonderful impression and influence on me. They certainly were a part of opening my heart and mind to Jesus. (My all-time favorite is "How Great Thou Art" and a close second is "Amazing Grace.")

- Trust Jesus Fully. Almost sixty years after meeting Jesus, everything they told me about him was true and more so.

Chapter 2
EVERY MORNING

"Who wouldn't want to start the day with the Lord of truth, love and forgiveness? This is living!"

The Sacred Hour

I f you were to encounter Chuck Reinhold during his senior year, you'd find a young man with a voracious hunger for anything of the Lord. He was a quick study in Scripture, prayer, and spending time caring for others, no matter where they were on their own faith journey. It was also during this time he learned how to take advantage of what would prove to be "the most important part" of his days.

Like David in Psalm 5, Chuck would be perfectly at home crying out, "In the morning, O LORD, you hear my voice; in the morning I lay my requests before you and wait in expectation."

Through the guidance of Bob Scott and my time in Campaigners, I learned the importance of meeting daily with the Lord. For me, this meant rising early in the morning, getting dressed, and sitting at my desk with my Bible.

There was no time more special than my early mornings with Jesus because it was here I learned to listen to the Spirit's counsel and recognize the great truths of God. And I was unapologetic about my passion on the topic!

How many hints, models, and commands does Scripture give us to start the day with the Lord?

Here is just one example.

In Mark 1:35 it says, "Very early in the morning, while it was still dark, Jesus got up, left the house and went off to a solitary place, where He prayed." How early? "*Very* ... while it was still dark."

Maybe it was *that* morning He agreed with His Father to die on the cross for our sins so we could have an eternal relationship with Him. Are we thankful Jesus got up early to hear His Father say that to Him?

The point is we should make a sufficient time in the morning before our regular day starts to meet with the Lord, to listen intensely to Him, and apply what He says to our lives: physically, mentally, socially, and spiritually. My guess is that if Jesus got up "very early," we should get up *very, very* early in the morning.

If you and I are eagerly meeting with the Lord "early" in the morning, I have no doubt those around us are enjoying a friendly, truthful, and forgiving person. And a person with many friends!

Who wouldn't become this kind of person when meeting early with the God of love, truth, and forgiveness every single morning?

In summary, I think of the Bible as "my best friend" in knowing and understanding the Lord and what He wants for my life.

I would need this supernatural counsel in the months to come as I considered the many attractive college scholarships coming my way…

Pitt's the Place!

Athletically speaking, my senior year (1957) picked up where junior year left off. I was at the top of my game in three sports: football (eighteen touchdowns my senior year), track (one of the state's best in the decathlon) and basketball (the starting point guard who helped lead the team to the divisional title). This six-foot one, 165-pound Mt. Lebanon Blue Devil was voted best athlete my senior year.

My athletic achievements at Mt. Lebanon would pay dividends for the next four years. Throughout 1956–1957, colleges up and down the East Coast came calling with football scholarships—Ohio State, Duke, Penn State, Pitt, and Harvard, to name just a few. I tried my best to handle the attention with maturity.

I was very thankful and humbled by it all, and it pressed me against the Lord. I prayed before every play for strength, courage, and to bless the team.

One assistant coach at Penn State by the name of Joe Paterno personally visited our home and invited me to visit the college. The experience impressed me, and I made Penn State my second option, but in my mind, first choice was a given—and for good reason.

Pitt was twenty minutes from my home. I would be able to remain near my Young Life leader, and Mt. Lebanon United Presbyterian Church, which were both very important to me. I've always been thankful for the Lord's guidance in this because I feel like the rest of my life was a result of that decision.

Another factor was the chance to be close to my family. Gwin was also grateful for this. "When Chuck played football at Pitt, the Pittsburgh papers loved the hometown boy and wrote about him often," she said. "I was an insecure teenager then and having a famous brother was not always easy. Chuck recognized I often felt like I was not good enough and couldn't measure up to him so, when he came home after a game, many times he would take his little sister's hand when walking someplace together. This filled me with pure joy, feeling so loved and accepted and valued for just me. And one more thing—I think he likes to be around me because I laugh uproariously at ALL his jokes!"

Bird Legs and Iron Mike

The years at Pitt were exciting, especially the times with the football team. The players lived in a very posh apartment tower, with large rooms, great service, and more food than we could possibly eat. I joined the Sigma Chi fraternity as did most of the football team.

The Pitt News ran a profile article on me my senior year, which began like this:

"They call him 'bird legs' because his legs are so thin. At 175 pounds, he is one of the Panthers' lightest men. But players and coaches alike will tell you that Chuck Reinhold is one of Pitt's top men on defense."

During my time at Pitt I became fast friends with teammate Mike Ditka, eventual NFL Hall of Famer, who along with the other linemen would open holes for the halfback known as "bird legs."

"Iron Mike" was tough yet nice. I had the privilege to take him to a Fellowship of Christian Athletes conference. Mike had a big heart and was open to knowing God!

The Boss

During my time at Pitt, Young Life was still very important to me. Throughout high school and college, I spent each summer at Frontier

Ranch, Young Life's camp in Buena Vista, Colorado. It was here I first met the man who founded the mission of Young Life, Jim Rayburn. He was simply a man, flawed like you and me, but one who loved Jesus and wanted teenagers to have that same opportunity. A true visionary leader, Jim was known fondly to the staff as "the boss."

I came to know Jim in a personal way. He invited me to spend time with him at his chalet and go with him on one of his afternoon climbs up the mountain. I consider it one of the most cherished experiences in my life. It took us all afternoon to climb up and come down that mountain and I loved every minute. Jim was very personal, and it became obvious to me why Young Life was effective in communicating the love of God to teenagers. There was nothing exceptional about the trip except that he was interested in me. He asked me about myself, my Young Life experience, and Pitt football. Wow!

Jim Rayburn built and trained Young Life staff on Jesus' command to "love one another." Jim continues to be one of my model/heroes. He built Young Life on Jesus Christ and His love and forgiveness. He also modeled starting the day with the Lord in Scripture and prayer. I cannot imagine the people who have been won to the Lord through his ministry... so many missionaries, ministers, people ministering in their families, neighborhoods, and workplaces. Thank you, Jim Rayburn!

PURE CHUCK (1961)

"My senior year I represented Sigma Chi in the annual Greek Festival, a huge event at the school. Most of the performers came dressed in suits prepared to deliver their monologues much like Johnny Carson. I showed up backstage dressed in a tutu, big army boots, leotard, and a belt. Of course, my two false front teeth were removed."

"My roommate, Eddie Clark, sat in the audience in complete fear, sure I was about to humiliate myself. I felt his fear as I compared myself to the others.

"My time came, and I ran across the stage screaming 'It's all around me. It's all around me.' The MC asked, 'What's all around you?' I screamed... 'My belt!' I had them at that moment, maybe my ridiculous outfit contributed, but the audience howled.

"I then recited 'Prinderella' (a tongue-twister mash-up of Cinderella) and ended up winning the comedy contest for my fraternity!"

—Chuck

Steeled for Change

In 1961, as my senior year wound down, I was again honored. That spring I received *The Pitt News Award*, considered the number one accolade offered to a graduating senior. This award recognized the athlete who best represented the school in the classroom, on the field, and in public.

I was shocked, embarrassed, happy, and thankful when my name was announced. I believe what put me over the top was my relationship with the Lord and His wonderful influence/leadership in my life.

Like my college decision four years earlier, I now faced an important crossroads on what step to take next. The Pittsburgh Steelers were well aware of my exploits as a hometown hero. Not wanting to waste a draft pick, they inquired if I would accept the offer if drafted.

As exciting as this once-in-a-lifetime opportunity appeared, my "steely" resolve was actually about to take me far, far away from Pittsburgh…

Principles Learned Along the Way

- A leader believes and demonstrates God's Word is his/her primary source of nourishment and his/her followers.
- Practice obedience. Meditating/listening with obedience to God's Word is the key to success. (Josh. 1:8)
- We should model the Navigators' "Wheel" illustration every meeting with individuals or groups in regard to:
  o Scripture
  o Prayer
  o Fellowship
  o Witnessing
  o Obedience to Jesus, or application

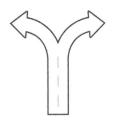

Chapter 3

LIVING THE WILD LIFE

"Obedience is the key to experiencing Jesus Christ."

The guest speaker wrapped up his sermon with this: "I'm going to an untouched tribe of people called the Anuaks in the wilds of lower Ethiopia. I'll need some help. Anyone want to volunteer?"

The year was 1961, the speaker was renowned missionary Don McClure, and the church was Mt. Lebanon Presbyterian. In the congregation that spring morning was one Charles Emerson Reinhold. You can guess the rest.

I had never felt God speaking to me so clearly. I don't think I even took time to think it through; I felt the Lord say, "go up and volunteer," which I did. I never looked back. I was happy to turn down the

Pittsburgh Steelers, no problem. I was so alive and happy to go on such an adventure with the Lord and this great man, Don McClure. I have never regretted that decision.

At the time, I had also been "hanging out" with another significant man of God. At twenty-two years old, I was devouring *Hudson Taylor's Spiritual Secret*, another major influence in my decision to join Don and his wife, Lyda. The objective of the trip would be this: I, along with three other young men, would travel to Ethiopia to help in the construction of a pioneer mission station among a tribe of 40,000 Anuaks.

Lions and Snakes and Crocs, Oh My!

Dave Phillips, Charlie Alcorn, and I boarded the S.S. Steel Seafarer freighter to Ethiopia on September 20, 1961. After thirty-one days, we happily stepped onto African soil, an eye-opening experience for three guys who'd never ventured outside the states.

Everything was different. The houses looked like they could fall apart in a storm. They were all made of branches and put together by I don't know what.

We met up with our fourth, Dave Brackenridge, in Addis Ababa and continued the westward trek to the other side of the country by means of jeep, small plane, and foot. The trip increased in difficulty the closer we came to our destination. Because there were no roads to where the Anuaks lived, we had to cut down trees and build makeshift bridges to cross streams. Although it could be exasperating work, the "road" trip also offered us a chance to be, well, boys.

Many times, a stream would go right across the road and, if it was a real big one, we would stop for a swim. How we loved the ice-cold streams compared to the hot weather.

By December 8, we had finally arrived at the Gila River near the Sudan border. Don McClure would be held up for another month because a local authority said he didn't have the right papers. The rest of us, all in our early twenties, were alone with the Anuaks... and a lot of wildlife.

While waiting for Don to arrive, we tried to keep it together, but we were scared to death. So, we said, "Okay, God, we're here for you, even if we have to be here the rest of our lives." We had a Young Life songbook and would walk and sing every day, then come back and work on the airstrip.

We did our best to set up camp. We spent weeks clearing out a lot of anthills as tall as we were to make room for that airfield. I killed thirteen venomous snakes the first week we were there. I lost count after that. They would stick their head out of a little hole in the huge anthills and spit venom. I hated it when that happened! I know why the Scripture compares Satan to a snake. They are sneaky and deadly.

We would encounter other animals in our eight-month stay including lions, elephants, leopards, water bucks, buffalo, pelicans, marabou storks, colobus monkeys, and, of course, crocodiles.

We saw a few people bitten by crocodiles with horrible injuries, yet Don allowed us to swim in the Gila River. We always had someone on the bank of the river with a gun. Don constantly reminded us that "God loves to be trusted!"

I didn't feel needy, yet we never had much of anything, including safety. This was living! I believed and experienced that "the Lord plus nothing was everything."

PURE CHUCK (1961)

"One night I heard a hissing sound coming from under my cot. I thought it was an aerosol can hissing and went to reach for it. I hesitated and then looked to see a puff adder snake curled up ready to strike. Needless to say, I quickly changed

*Chuck, the one with the hearts on his shorts,
working hard to tear down the ant hills.*

*Always humorous, Chuck took a long time staging this photo of little kids
pretending they were the "work crew" clearing the ant hills.*

my plan and managed to kill it. That was the first of many puff adder kills. We got them before they got us.

Chuck has always loved animals and nature, and this domesticated Cheetah was no different. He loved his friend's pet cheetah!

"I had many experiences of being humbled by the greatness of God. It got so I would just take walks alone into the Savannah, trusting God to protect me. I would sing and pray as I walked. One day I came upon a lion, but he just looked at me and kept walking. My wife, Linda, told me the lion probably saw huge angels walking with me. I thought it was because he thought I was too skinny."

—**Chuck**

Giving Them the Best

The tribe was friendly, poor, and eager to receive anything missionaries could give them. Long lines of sick Anuaks waited for medical care. Don was not a doctor, but dressed in his white shirt and shorts, he did what he could. Penicillin was miraculous for their cuts and infections.

One evening, he called us from our tent and told us to follow him to the village where a witch doctor was attempting to heal a sick woman. She danced all around the fire, put her hands in it, and then grabbed the woman around her neck. It was frightening!

Later, the sick woman came to Don, who helped her get well. A testimony to the power of God.

While the people were needy for many things, Don gave them the best—Jesus Christ. Seeing Don teach the Gospel under a huge banyan tree was thrilling to me.

The most wonderful thing I learned from Don McClure was that the Word of God contained our message and was our authority. I've always appreciated that he gave our Lord Jesus Christ and the Scriptures full credit for all he accomplished. Don and Lyda were my examples of the most wonderful people God ever created. They loved the Lord and found the abundant life He promised by following Him.

[Don McClure would continue his missionary efforts in Ethiopia for the next sixteen years. He was shot and killed by Somali guerrillas on March 27, 1977. He became the first entrant in the book of Presbyterian martyrs.]

A Walk to Remember

By May 1962, it was time to leave and we had two choices: 1) We could fly out, which would take only one day, or 2) we could walk out with our dear Anuak friends, a trek of several weeks through uncharted ground, filled with snakes and all the rest.

It was no contest. We chose to walk with our friends.

The reasoning? It pressed us against our Lord, which was real living. Yeah!

We started the journey at night to avoid the sun's oppressive heat.

It was scary. Who would have thought the night trip would take us through a swamp up to our shoulders in water (and whatever)? I still think of it as an experience with the Lord more than a slog through a swamp. *He loves to be trusted.* I'm sure the Lord was preparing me for the next great adventure in my life with Him.

What this would be had been weighing heavily on my heart and mind all spring. As I began to make plans for leaving the Gila River mission station, I received a letter from my sister Gwin, saying she was going to a Young Life weekend camp.

In Ethiopia, I had seen a huge God who took away my fear. I had prayed every day, "Lord, what's the most important thing I could do for you?" Up to that point I didn't have a clue what I would do when I got back home, but Gwin's letter was more than a clue. The Lord spoke loud and clear to me from that letter that high schools were lost tribes and Young Life was a mission to them. I thought about how thankful I was that Bob Scott came to my high school and led me to the Lord through Young Life.

I asked myself three questions:

- Was doing Young Life scary?
- Were high schools lost tribes?
- Should I then go there?

The answer to all three questions? A resounding "Yes!"

I'm absolutely positive God took me to Ethiopia to help me see the lost tribe of teenagers, a tribe that has few missionaries. I wrote to Harry McDonald, the area director in Pittsburgh at the time, and said, "I want to come on Young Life staff. Is there a place for me?"

Principles Learned Along the Way

- God loves to be trusted! It was in the lowlands of Ethiopia I experienced Jesus is truly "life and life abundant."

- A leader believes and demonstrates nothing is done except through prayer and the Holy Spirit. Learn to pray without ceasing. God will never leave you or forsake you.
- Love without words. Living among natives who did not speak my language taught me one of the great lessons of life as I learned to love without words. (1 John 3:18)

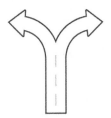

Chapter 4
A LIFELONG PIONEER

*"Having to get out of my car and walk toward
that high school pressed me against the Lord."*

Pioneer [pahy-*uh*-**neer**]
noun

1. a person who is among those who first enter or settle a region, thus opening it for occupation and development by others.
2. one who is first or among the earliest in any field of inquiry, enterprise, or progress.

Chuck Reinhold embodies both of these definitions. Since his return from Ethiopia in the spring of 1962, he's always been a pioneer, be it starting a new club, new area, new way to train staff, or even new work in a foreign country.

Chuck received a response to his letter to Harry McDonald. Yes, there was indeed a place in Young Life for Chuck—and that place was Baltimore.

The Wrong Profession?

My first assignment with the mission was to start Young Life clubs in both Woodlawn and Dundalk High Schools. It was not uncommon in the early days of Young Life for staff to be running clubs at multiple schools—in fact, it was often assumed. Nor was it uncommon for the schools to be located some distance from one another. This was certainly true in my case: Woodlawn and Dundalk lay on opposite sides of the city of Baltimore.

Added to the external challenges of time and distance were internal feelings of inadequacy—feelings to which many Young Life staff and volunteers can attest. The idea of going to a high school and trying to meet disinterested kids, while not as life-threatening as swimming with Ethiopian crocodiles, can still produce an intense fear. For me, the self-proclaimed introvert, the prospect was often terrifying.

I remember driving to the high school, getting out of the car, taking a few steps toward the high school, then panicking, getting back into the car and driving around the block praying for courage and the Lord's guidance and then trying again.

It was so scary that I had difficulty remembering the details of my contact work at the schools. I do remember my skin would break out in hives and I was sent to a psychiatrist. After a few consultations, he explained my body was telling me I was in the wrong profession.

This shocked me to my core, but a pattern quickly emerged that would follow me throughout my life. When confronted with a challenge, such as this notion of leaving the ministry to which God had obviously called me, I responded like my Savior in the desert: I countered with Scripture.

I found out early on how important it was to steep my mind in God's Word, and the best way to do that is through memorizing it daily. In fact, I often recited these verses on the way to the high school—it was a great way to speak to my fears. This was to become a lifelong discipline for me, and I'm so thankful I learned it early.

It's funny, I guess, but that doctor's diagnosis was what convinced me Young Life was the right place for me. I'd recently memorized one of my favorite verses, John 15:5, which says, "I am the vine; you are the branches. If a man remains in me, and I in Him, he will bear much fruit; apart from me you can do nothing." Jesus Christ meant everything to me and having to get out of my car and walk toward that high school pressed me against the Lord. I don't think I took one step without a prayer for His presence, guidance, and courage.

Along with His Word, the Lord also encouraged me through a seemingly unlikely class. A man on the committee encouraged me, at twenty-three years old, to enroll in the Dale Carnegie Public Speaking Course. Each week I would give a three- to five-minute talk and then learn from the instructor's critique. It was one of the greatest things to happen in my life.

I was also required to read the book *How to Win Friends and Influence People*. The book was a treasure to me, helping me to know how to obey the Lord's command to love others as He has loved us.

One principle within the book stated: *Remember that a person's name is to that person the sweetest sound in any language.*

I worked hard to apply this to my ministry in Young Life. I worked hard at remembering kids' names, writing them down, and reviewing them at night. I can still remember the delighted expression on kids' faces when I smiled and said "hi" to them by name; and in working hard at remembering their names, I fell in love with them.

Another Carnegie principle was talking *in terms of the other person's interests.*

I—and thousands of Young Life staff and volunteers like me—have used this idea to know kids and learn how best to care for them. Over the decades, we've cultivated the art of asking questions and finding out what's important to the kids we're trying to befriend. This builds bridges with kids and informs a staff person on their often-changing culture.

Do I think this book had any influence on my Young Life ministry? My club at Woodlawn grew from 30 kids to 300. We had to meet in a church hall because we didn't have a house big enough.

Among the initial thirty there was one kid in particular whose name and interests would become of primary importance to me—a Woodlawn sophomore named Linda Carroll...

My first club on Young Life staff was significant in ways I would not learn until later. The club was not only my first as a leader, but the first for Linda Carroll, who had been invited by some of her upper-class girlfriends.

"I had no idea what Young Life was," Linda said, "but because they invited me, it was a big deal. The club was exciting because of all the kids there. There was singing and a skit where I proceeded to rub black soot all over my face in what is known as 'The Hypnotist Skit.' After many laughs and much embarrassment on my part, we all quieted down. The former leader, Jerry Johnson, began introducing this very handsome guy, Chuck Reinhold.

"Little did I know how much my life was about to change. I remember to this day the ski sweater Chuck wore and his blonde hair, yes, hair he still had. Chuck spoke from the Bible and told us a story about Jesus. My impression of Jesus was mostly the baby Jesus born on Christmas."

Her first time at Young Life club left an indelible impression. Linda was hooked.

That fall she attended the Young Life Baltimore weekend camp in Natural Bridge, Virginia. As the weekend in Bedford Springs, Pennsylvania, did for me, so this time brought out the uninhibited exploits of youth in Linda.

"It was an eight-hour bus ride," she remembered, "and I don't think I had ever had more fun, especially smoking cigars in the back of the bus. [Obviously unbeknownst to her leaders!] When we arrived at the hotel, somehow three of my best friends and I were in a room without a counselor. This was a big mistake. The first night we rolled toilet paper down the hallway and stairs to the lobby."

Also mirroring my first weekend experience was the spiritual change Linda realized over the course of the three days. "The speaker was Carl Nelson. During the cross talk, Carl made the message real; I had never heard what Jesus went through that day. I was sad and ashamed."

That night, Linda and her friends forgot all about repeating the previous night's pranks and went straight back to their room for a frank discussion on the message they'd heard. Linda soon sensed that they were not alone. "All of a sudden I got scared and was afraid to look in the corner of our room where a huge wardrobe stood.

A photo of Linda Carroll (Reinhold) in high school on her way to a dance at Woodlawn.

I was convinced Jesus was standing there with His arms wide open, waiting for me. It was the first time I ever realized Jesus was real!"

The next morning, I approached Linda and asked her if she'd received Christ into her heart.

"I told Chuck, 'I think so,' and he was thrilled! This was a new beginning for me in every way. I began going to Campaigners and studying the Bible for the first time."

Chuck E's in Love

Time passed, and with it, Linda's high school years. I decided to take this college-bound lady out on our first date—a day trip in my green Volkswagen bug to the National Zoo in Washington, D.C.

"It was the most romantic day of my life, a dream come true," Linda said. "After dinner, we walked around the Tidal Basin, holding hands and dreaming about the future.

"The Lord told me very clearly I was going to love and care for Chuck and be his helper in ministry. It was such a strong message and one I delighted in. I was thrilled to be called by God to love this man!"

- -

PURE CHUCK (circa 1960s)

"Over time, Chuck invited me to play basketball with him and his buddies. Wow. He was quick. We became great friends and competitors with the two of us nearly coming to blows at Star Ranch during a heated one-on-one duel, which I typically lost. I loved his competitive spirit.

"I did have an advantage over him in lacrosse though. What irony. A champion collegiate football great was placed by Young Life into Baltimore County, where there was no football, only lacrosse. Imagine, no football in Baltimore County schools! God has a sense of humor and Charles

Emerson Reinhold was the brunt of it. The only thing funnier than watching Chuck attempt golf was to watch him play lacrosse. So humbling."

—**Doug Holladay**, former Young Life staff and
Special Ambassador under President Reagan

From Woodlawn to the World!

My three years in Baltimore changed not only the trajectory of Linda's life, but those of many other students as well. One such student, Harry Perrine, recounts the ripple effect our high bar for discipleship eventually produced around the globe:

"I was invited to Campaigners to learn more about how to be a Christ follower. We met every Sunday around 3 o'clock in the afternoon. It was there I discovered how passionate Chuck was about his faith in Christ, and how compelled he was to transfer that passion and devotion to us kids, maybe twenty-five or thirty in attendance.

"One Sunday I missed Campaigners and Chuck caught up with me after school on Monday. He said, 'Where were you yesterday? I missed you.' To which I replied, 'I had homework to do and had to miss it.' Wrong answer. Chuck said, 'You do what you want to do. If you really wanted to be at Campaigners, you would have scheduled out your time and completed your homework on Friday night or Saturday. You do what you want to do.' Ouch! That hurt! I never missed another meeting.

"Eventually we started praying for students and teachers every morning at the school. We would go to the stairwell which led up to the roof and stop at a landing, and each morning we would gather there, maybe ten or fifteen of us, and pray like mad. It was absolutely cool to see God working so mightily.

"I remember one Campaigners where Chuck quoted Acts 1:8, where Jesus said, 'But you will receive power when the Holy Spirit comes on you; and you will be my witnesses in Jerusalem, and in all Judea and Samaria, and to the ends of the earth.' He asked us, 'Do you believe this verse?' All of us kind of sheepishly said 'yeah,' because we knew it was the right answer—but deep down inside we were very doubtful and uncertain. How could a bunch of high school kids be witnesses to the ends of the earth? That is probably not going to happen. That being said, looking back over the last fifty plus years, that verse has come true over and over again.

"The influence and impact that little group of about thirty or so Campaigners has had on this planet is almost staggering. Let me list some of the people who have gone on to share the wonderful news of Jesus Christ and how life changing He is. These are just some of the people from that little group:

- Dick Bond—*Young Life staff, now pastor*
- Andy Byrd—*Young Life staff*
- Linda Carroll Reinhold—*Young Life staff (U.S. and Ethiopia)*
- Michael Coleman—*Young Life staff, now pastor*
- Joni Eareckson Tada—*Founder of Joni and Friends, has written dozens of books and devotionals, traveled and spoken all over the world*
- Newt Hetrick—*Young Life staff, founder of International English and Cultural Studies*
- Doug Holladay—*Young Life staff, served under President Reagan in the state department*
- Betsy Sandbower—*Young Life staff (U.S. and Europe)*
- Ray Steckman—*Young Life staff, retired teacher*

- Me—*Volunteer Young Life leader and committee chairman, founding elder of LifePoint Church with two thousand in attendance*

"I guess we really didn't believe Acts 1:8 then, but we sure believe it now. We've all lived it to the fullest extent. And the verse goes on and on, because we all have asked the kids and adults we try to influence the very same question. 'Do you believe that verse?' Same response. But you know what? They're experiencing the same result! And that is great news. All because a man so in love with Jesus Christ came to our high school and loved on us like no other and shared with us the wonderful and exciting news of the person of Jesus Christ. Thanks, Chuck!"

Principles Learned Along the Way...

- Remember names. "Remember that a person's name is to that person the sweetest and most important sound in any language." —Dale Carnegie
- "Talk in terms of the other person's interests." —Dale Carnegie
- You do what you want to do. (In other words, you make time for what's important to you.) Does your weekly schedule reflect this?

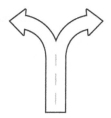

Chapter 5

"THE" CITY

"Am I doing things I wouldn't try without Christ?"

W hen a Young Life club grows from 30 to 300 kids, most leaders would be beside themselves with happiness. "Surely the Lord's hand is upon this," they might think. Throw in a beautiful girlfriend who'll be a freshman at a local college, and it would seem perfectly natural to want to put down roots in Baltimore for years to come.

"He always thought of himself as a pioneer missionary," Linda said, "and he was eager to go to an area that didn't have Young Life. He had a vision to develop the nearby cities and states."

Chuck shared his vision to again start something new with a few of the Baltimore volunteer leaders, Craig "Gorgo" Laferty, Bo White, and

Bill Linthicum. "Chuck wanted us to commit our hearts to finding a city and then go there in faith to start Young Life," Craig said. "But how was that going to happen? We prayed. We drove to cities to scout them out. We prayed some more."

Around this time, a man by the name of Kent Woodworth contacted Young Life's headquarters and asked the mission to send staff to Rochester to start the work there. "The request was passed along to Chuck," Craig said, "and he began looking at the map of Upstate New York. He saw these cities all lined up along Interstate 90: Buffalo, Rochester, Syracuse, Utica, Albany. It reminded him of the unreached places in Ethiopia."

In Chuck's heart, there was only one conclusion—Rochester was "the" city.

Ground Chuck

By 1965 the vision was taking shape. I began recruiting leaders, and like the Campaigners group back at Woodlawn High School, the team would become a "who's who" in Young Life and beyond. I gathered the best and the brightest: Judy Weber Smathers served on staff, while Rochester Institute of Technology (RIT) undergrads Bill Updike, Bill Linthicum, and Greg Kinberg also joined in the effort.

The five men—me, the two Bills, a Craig, and a Greg—decided to live in a house together. We called the cottage "The Whetstone House" because, in Old Testament times, a whetstone was used to sharpen iron, a reference to Prov. 27:17—"As iron sharpens iron, so one person sharpens another."

The community built during those years bore witness both to my leadership strengths and domestic weaknesses.

"We had the idea we would model Christian living together, even in sharing chores," Craig said. "We each had a night that was our night to cook. Some of us were okay, but Chuck was bad. His idea of a 'home cooked meal' was to brown a chuck of ground beef, add five cans of

Campbell's vegetable soup, mix it together, and call that a meal. We joked about that all the time—and tried to avoid it as well!

"Chuck was the engine and glue behind Young Life taking hold in Rochester. He demonstrated how to reach out to kids, love them, and 'win the right to be heard.' He set the standard in having a dynamic Young Life club and a ministry to an entire high school. And along the way, we always had lots of laughs."

Linda's initial times in Rochester, however, did not prove as jovial as mine.

Reunited (Twice)

After spending her freshman year studying at Catonsville Community College, Linda pined for her pioneer (as I did her). Deciding she'd transfer schools to be close to me, she enrolled at Roberts Wesleyan College, about ten miles southwest of downtown Rochester and began her studies there in the fall of 1966.

For the nineteen-year-old who knew no one at the school, "Roberts Wesleyan was very conservative, very strict, and very lonely. Having come from almost no church background, but having a vital relationship with the Lord, made it difficult for me and others. I didn't speak the same lingo and I loved being around non-believers. I was definitely out of my element."

True, Linda was now in the same city as me, but conflicting schedules and Linda's lack of transportation severely cut down on our time together; when we did see each other, it was primarily on the weekends. She started reflecting on our relationship.

"One day I came to the conclusion Chuck and I should break up. I remember thinking I needed to know the Lord apart from Chuck. He had been my entire 'Christian' experience up to now. Later, I went to the school chapel and began crying: I prayed the Lord would take away my feelings for Chuck."

The most difficult thing, she said, was telling me. "You were so surprised! You were sad, but I knew it was important to follow through. I was now free to make relationships with other students and not feel torn inside because of you. I became excited about being a part of the student body; I also began wearing more makeup than ever before. It was crazy, but it was my way of saying you could be a Christian and still be in the world."

After several months apart, Linda and I began seeing each other again. We picked up right where we had left off. A month after rekindling the relationship, I took Linda walking along the shore of Lake Ontario.

"All of a sudden Chuck stopped and said, 'Look, a bottle with a note in it!' This bottle was stuck in the sand as though it had drifted to this beach. I opened it at Chuck's urging and began reading it. I suddenly realized it was Chuck asking me to marry him."

The "two became one" within three months, on September 2, 1967. We were married at a local Presbyterian church by Charlie Alcorn, my best friend who accompanied me on the Ethiopia trip five years earlier.

In typical Young Life fashion, the wedding was most definitely not a somber affair. "Our car had 'It's a skit' written all over it," Linda said.

After a honeymoon in Bermuda, the happy couple hit the ground running.

"We went straight to a Young Life staff conference in Hershey, Pennsylvania," Linda said. "Being newlyweds and coming straight from our honeymoon, you can imagine all the snickering and comments. Here I was with all these legends of Young Life and their wives and I'd just turned twenty a few days before our wedding."

Returning home, Linda stood alongside me in the work, serving leaders, holding Bible studies with committee women and, of course, ministering to kids.

Chuck and Linda's wedding day!

From Gritted Teeth to Gratitude

To see the influence in four years in Rochester, one need look no further than three young men and their specific interactions with me. The first was Greg Kinberg, a student at RIT in 1965.

"I became a Christian through Young Life in my senior year of high school," Greg said. "I had no clue I should seek God in choosing a college and chose to go halfway across the country to Rochester to go to school. My girlfriend wrote me that summer from Trail West to tell me she had just met the guy who would be starting Young Life in Rochester that fall."

When Greg arrived at RIT, he and I connected immediately. We started to meet regularly, and I suggested we go through the Navigators' *Topical Memory System* and the *Growing in Christ* series together. "That was over the top 'Sunday School legalism' to me," Greg said, "but I really enjoyed time with Chuck, so I said, 'Sure.'"

We met the next week, but Greg had not kept up his end of the bargain. "When Chuck discovered I hadn't memorized my verse or done the lesson, he ended the time and told me to call him when I got it done and wanted to get together. I was so mad. So mad."

While Greg stewed, a fellow student told him I could be very strong but was doing it out of my concern for Greg and his relationship with Christ. "So, I did the lesson and memorized the verse and we met," Greg said. "It was the beginning of a four-year discipleship relationship I will forever be grateful for. Chuck is my spiritual father and a paragon in my spiritual life."

PURE CHUCK (circa 1960s)

"Speaking of Scripture memory and the earliest of days in Rochester, Chuck had two incidents worth mentioning. Twice he had accidents in his little green Volkswagen beetle (the car that all Young Life staff drove in those days). Pulling into a gas station and up to a pump while looking at a TMS verse, he ran into a gas pump and dented the fender—no harm to the pump. Not long after that he rear-ended Steve Walther, a popular junior at the school because, once again, he was memorizing Scripture as he drove. (An earlier equivalent of texting while driving!) Interesting way to meet kids—Steve did end up coming to Young Life club."

—**Tuck Knupp**

Dishes, Homework, and Jesus

Through my guidance, a second young man named Terry learned how to take the Lord at His Word. I shared about our encounter in a sermon years later:

Terry had just committed his life to Christ, and he was thrilled. Everybody saw the change in Terry. He was a wild kid—not living for very much, except the weekends. And Christ changed his life.

A little bit later on he called me up and said, "Chuck, it's not working." And I could hear his voice quivering and quaking. He said, "I'm going to run away from home. I just wanted you to know about it. I wanted to say goodbye."

I said, "Terry, why don't you come on over, and let's talk about it."

So, he came over and about the first thing he said was, "Well, I don't want to hear anything about praying and reading the Bible! It worked at first, and I was never so happy. Christ is not real."

"Well, Terry, would you like Jesus Christ to be real in your life the way He was?"

"I would."

So, we talked some more, and I shared this passage in John 14:21: "Whoever has my commands and keeps them is the one who loves me. The one who loves me will be loved by my Father, and I too will love them and show myself to them."

"Terry what does that mean?" We talked about it. "Jesus is promising here that He will make Himself known to us if we keep His commandments. Terry, do you really want to have the reality of Christ in your life?"

"Yes."

"Okay, what areas do you need to obey Christ in, and you're ignoring, or running from?"

The first thing he said was he just can't stand his mother. She is constantly nagging him about one thing and another, and he just can't live in that house another second.

"Terry, how could you obey God and honor your mother and love her? What would you never do if Jesus Christ was not in your life?"

And he thought about that, and this shocked me, but he said, "The dishes." And he had tears in his eyes. He was serious. He said, "I would never do the dishes. Boy, I never have. And it would be plain humiliating for me to do it now."

"You never do it on your own?"

"No, it would be impossible."

"Well, what would it be like if you went home, had dinner and then just got up and did the dishes? If you stuck your hands in the water, and thanked God for everything you can think of—warm soapy water, the dishes, the food that was on it, the house, your parents—and do the dishes with the Lord? Terry, the last couple of weeks you have not done anything that you really needed Christ to do. And that is why it has not been real. What else would you never do, Terry, if Christ were not in your life?"

"Study. I am so far behind now, it would not really do any good."

"After dinner, why don't you go upstairs, clean off your desk, sit down with the Lord, and study? Begin to read, and when you have to remember something, say, 'Lord, help me remember this.' Concentrate, and just have a good time with the Lord. You want to try it, Terry?"

He was all for it, and I could tell he was getting excited. We prayed together, and he left.

The next morning, about nine o' clock, his mother called.

"Was Terry over there last night?"

"He was."

"You know he is such a sloppy kid." That was her opener. "You know, he got up from the table last night and did the dishes and he did them perfectly. He has never done that before. And then he went upstairs and studied." She just wanted me to know that.

That afternoon, I heard pounding and my doorbell ringing. Terry was standing there, a big smile on his face. "Chuck, I spent the happiest night of my life last night. I did the dishes and studied."

I said, "Is Christ real to you?"

"You bet."

"Do you believe the promise of God?"

"I do."

His life was changed. He got back on track of launching out into the deep where Christ is, for that is where God has called us…

On Chuck and Tuck

Perhaps no teen in Rochester has gone on to walk through more of life with me than Dave "Tuck" Knupp. The Irondequoit High School junior met me and was immediately impressed with this man who possessed "an enthusiasm and humor like no one else" he'd ever met. (Of course, I credit all that to the Lord.)

I enlisted Tuck to go to Frontier Ranch in August of 1965, and Tuck in turn enlisted nine of his friends. Not one of the ten had ever seen a Young Life club and none had a relationship with Christ. The week at camp was a turning point for Tuck.

"When I returned from Frontier," Tuck said, "a dramatic change had occurred in my life as a result of my new faith in Christ."

His parents couldn't help but notice the change, Tuck said, and they were intrigued. "Mom and Dad were very active in the local Presbyterian church but didn't have much of an informed faith. They invited Chuck for dinner, so they could get to know my new friend and mentor and learn more about this Young Life thing. (By the way, Young Life was small and not very well known in those days. When the possibility arose for me to go to Frontier, my dad called the FBI to check this group out! He finally got the green light from one of our former pastors who knew of Young Life.)"

I spent many dinners with the Knupp family and the discussions covered everything from faith to football.

Tuck said, "My dad found his own faith strangely growing from the times he spent with Chuck. Later on, my dad would remark, 'I never knew anyone to talk about the Lord with such genuine enthusiasm, but then I was a bit taken aback when he used the same tone of voice to talk about Vince Lombardi!'

"Chuck's enthusiasm was absolutely contagious, whether he was talking about Jesus or the UCLA basketball team or how to make the best possible cup of coffee."

The Knupps hosted the very first Rochester Young Life club in the fall of 1965; that night 100 kids packed into a house which had never held that many bodies. Not surprisingly, club soon outgrew the Knupps' residence and by the end of that fall, the number of kids showing up had doubled.

From the beginning, we brought the Campaigner kids in on the ministry.

"Chuck would regularly explain to me why he was doing what he was doing, the methodology of it, and how to think about things," said Tuck. "I distinctly remember how he pulled me aside one day and explained why he was up at the school and what he was trying to accomplish (contact work). I felt like a real insider!"

Chuck gave the Campaigners ownership of the club. Tuck explained. "That meant having a prayer list of people we wanted to invite, loving them, extending ourselves to them, and eventually, when the time was right, inviting them to club and offering them a ride. We were taught to sit in the middle of club and help make the skits successful by laughing hard. We were to sing the songs enthusiastically and listen intently to the speaker. Greeting new kids and reluctant kids was also an expectation. No one was a spectator; whether or not club was successful was the responsibility of all of us, not just the people leading from up front.

"In our little Campaigner group Chuck was a stickler for 'no negative humor.' If you ever got sarcastic or poked fun at someone else, you could expect to be reprimanded. Faith in Christ always meant building one another up and encouraging one another."

Why did the kids respond so well?

Tuck credits it to passion. "When it came to motivating others to be their best in Christ I don't think I've ever met anyone like Charles Emerson Reinhold. 'I mean, really, why would you *ever even want* to do anything else?' might be the kind of thing he would punctuate a particular teaching with.

"Nobody could make you feel as good about yourself or as ready to run through trees and parked cars to get to the high school than Chuck. I consider him to be the premier discipler I've ever met."

Principles Learned Along the Way

- Giving Campaigners ownership in the ministry grew their faith tremendously.
- Processing "along the way" is the most effective classroom.
- Ministry is not a spectator sport; everyone needs to take the field!

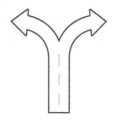

Chapter 6

TRANSITION, TRAGEDY, AND TRAINING

"A Graduate School for Christ!"

I have this recurring dream of a trained Young Life staff person walking down the sidewalk and a couple standing across the street notices him/her. The one says to the other, "There goes a great man of God." The other says, "He is on Young Life staff." I like the idea that the first impression was their life in Christ, but yet their skill in directing the Young Life ministry was also noticed and valued. My dream is that our staff could be parachuted down anywhere in the world, and they would immediately go to work mobilizing people to draw kids to maturity in Christ. They would have both the attractiveness of the life of Christ and the leadership and management skills to get the job done.

By 1969, Chuck was on the move again. Tom Raley, the Eastern Divisional Director, and a man who'd been involved with Young Life since the early days, asked Chuck to consider moving to the D.C. area to begin a training program for new staff. As was the case in the move from Baltimore, the Reinholds could think of many reasons to turn down the offer and stay in Rochester. But the trailblazer knew he must go, and he and Linda moved south.

"Tom wanted us to live in Montgomery County," Linda remembered, "because there was already a great history of Young Life with a wonderful committee and leaders. But once again, Chuck's pioneering spirit kicked in and he chose Prince George's County, where there was no Young Life."

Embracing Diversity at DuVal

I immediately plunged into the work at DuVal High School, located outside the beltway, northeast of D.C. "Chuck picked up a ministry Fred Harrison had started and almost immediately turned it into the most incredibly huge, multi-racial club most had ever seen," said Tuck, who came on staff after graduating from Duke and followed the Reinholds to Prince George's County.

"The African American kids were key to the whole club," Linda added. "What was most exciting was the vision these kids had for the rest of the high school. They invited the white kids and club grew so big we had to meet above the fire hall."

"One night the leaders invited the DuVal Drill Team to come and perform at club," Tuck recalled. "That team was made up entirely of African American girls and when they were done, the entire club went wild with applause and approval. It brought the races together in that school and you could tell those girls had never felt such appreciation in all their lives."

Dave Miller, a key kid at the school, had a front row seat to the exciting changes at DuVal. "Young Life remained racially inclusive in a high school that was very racially divided, and after one year, club topped over 300 kids!"

It's important to note, Dave said, that while I was an outstanding leader, I was also quite human. "This became clear to me through my college years when Chuck somehow twisted my arm to join him on the Wallace Presbyterian Church basketball team. Now, we all know Chuck can be intense, but I was a little surprised when, after the opening tip-off, the opponent fouled Chuck as he went in for a layup. Chuck came down on his feet, turned to his opponent and proceeded to strangle him by the neck! But of course, by the middle of third quarter Chuck was leading this person to Christ!

"Yes, at times it was hard to handle Chuck's constant intensity," Dave continued. "But thanks be to God for Linda. Whether discipling a group of girls in club, enriching a conversation with her gracious and sweet spirit, offering a listening ear, or providing a home that was always welcoming, Linda always seemed to find a way to complement Chuck. In every ministry and in every season of life. No doubt about it, Linda has always been part and parcel of all of Chuck's accomplishments in ministry. Linda Reinhold is a 'helpmate extraordinaire!'"

Sweet Corrie

My helpmate extraordinaire discovered she was pregnant during our second year of ministry at DuVal in 1969. "The club girls were all so happy for me," Linda said. "Keep in mind that I wasn't that much older than they were."

Celebrating the joyous news with the many who loved us, Linda and I were the beneficiaries of at least six baby showers. At one particular shower in Baltimore, the spouses were also invited. Making an appearance there was none other than the current Vice President, Spiro T. Agnew. "He and his wife were among my parents' closest friends. I have a great picture of a very pregnant me sitting on Uncle Spiro's lap!" Linda said.

"Linda was made to be a mother," remembered Tuck, who was living with the Reinholds at the time. "No one was more wired that way than she was—and now, finally, they were expecting their first."

Linda went into labor during a leadership retreat in Maryland, and I whisked her to Providence Hospital in D.C.

"It was a long labor that went through the night," Tuck said. "That next day all of the trainees in the whole D.C. area and other staff were supposed to take a bus tour, where we stopped and prayed at each school around the Beltway. Before I left for the bus that morning the phone rang; it was Chuck, who simply said, 'Tuck, the baby died at birth, would you please tell the rest?'

"I'll never forget those words. Little Corrie, a perfectly formed baby girl died due to complications and stress from the long labor. An unspeakable tragedy."

Linda and I held Corrie for a long time. It's the first time I remember crying as an adult. Sadly, it was before cell phones and we don't even have a picture of her, but we know where she is and where to find her. She's in heaven with our Lord Jesus and so many wonderful people.

"She was beautiful!" Linda said. "Her face will always be in my mind. Chuck and I prayed and thanked the Lord for His will and plans."

"It is hard to imagine how painful that must have been for them," Tuck said. "It is a mystery that we still cannot fully understand, but God often shapes his favorites through intense suffering."

The Young Life Training Program

After nearly a decade working with kids, I was thrilled to begin thinking about what a Young Life training program for new staff might look like.

From my earliest days on staff I had given considerable thought and prayer to what someone must embrace to enter into the mission.

I, of course, didn't come up with these ideas alone, nor did I develop them in some ivory tower. They evolved over the years of working side by side with the men and women I loved.

Four such men were Doug Holladay, Greg Kinberg, Skip Ryan, and Brad Smith, who comprised the inaugural class in 1969. These Young Life trainees (a term no longer in vogue, by the way) covered a large swath of mission field: Brad and Greg were placed in nearby Montgomery County, Maryland, while Doug and Skip worked in areas in Northern Virginia.

The following year, the D.C. Training Program tripled in size with the addition of eight more trainees: Dick Bond, George Kennedy, Tuck Knupp, Don Lemons, Steve Oliver, Gary Treichler, Bo White, and Bill Zierden.

"Now there were a dozen different personalities when we met every Friday for training," Tuck said. "The emphasis on becoming men in Christ always took priority over the techniques of running Young Life ministry, although both were addressed each week. The format was learning by discovery, but most of us learned early on that Chuck had a pretty clear idea of what exactly it was we were supposed to discover!

"As always, Chuck was strong on Navigator materials. Accountability was high. We had assignments each week and were always checked on our homework. The full Topical Memory System, all sixty verses, was expected to be completed by the end of the two years."

Each trainee was expected to run two clubs, Campaigners, and, in some cases, a leadership meeting as well. The mixture of camaraderie, enthusiasm, and relative inexperience in running an area made for exciting times… and for a great deal of introspection.

"The insecurity of comparison was an issue for most of us," Tuck recalled. "Each week as we shared, it seemed like everyone else in the room was doing better than I was—something more creative, more successful, etc. Chuck was, I think, the only one not impressed or caught up in all of this ministry comparison. He always had a laser-like focus on who we were becoming in Christ and that was really the only important thing to him."

"It was a great team," Linda recalls, "and Chuck loved all of them. This was a very profound time for him as he developed so many of his core ideas for training. By this time, Tom Raley had promoted Chuck to Metro Director over all of D.C., Montgomery, Prince George's, Fairfax, Arlington, and Loudoun Counties. The trainees had clubs all over. Skip Ryan started the first club at Yorktown High School, which is where our kids would one day go!"

Like so many in the history of missions, our work would eventually, to paraphrase one of our Lord's parables, grow to produce a crop—thirty, sixty, or even a hundred times what was sown.

PURE CHUCK (circa 1990s)

"We had a five-week assignment at Lake Champion together and during that time we had Russian students come to camp. One of their chaperones was Boris, a KGB agent. He brought gifts to give us. He gave us a big jar of caviar. I remember Chuck scooped a heaping tortilla chip of caviar, put it into his mouth, and then teared up. He stole my Sprite and downed it. Then he ran to the kitchen and put his head under the sink."

—**Randy Nickel**, longtime Young Life staff

"Soon Chuck would hand over the reins of Prince George's County to Tuck," Dave Miller said. "Tuck did a terrific job building a team of fifty-plus volunteer leaders and five thriving Young Life clubs. Chuck's influence would continue to be felt in subsequent Prince George's County area directors, including Lee Corder, Pat Goodman, Mike O'Leary, Rick Rogan, and Mark Johnson."

Principles Learned Along the Way

- "Make the last word His Word!"
- "Every club kid walks around with a sign around his neck that says, 'I want to be appreciated.'"
- "Never expect people to act like Christians until they've met Christ!"

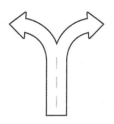

THE TRAINING PROGRAM DOCUMENT

By Chuck Reinhold

While Chuck began the Young Life Training Program as early as 1969, he spent the next two decades tweaking his "Graduate School for Christ." What follows is a later version that encompasses his vision and desire for each young staff man and woman...

The "Graduate School for Christ" was developed to make everyone realize what we were doing in Young Life was for Jesus Christ. Young Life was the vehicle. It gave people the training to go beyond a "college degree" in Christ. And the great thing about working in Young Life was it taught us so much about how to live for Jesus Christ and be obedient to Him. To be effective in Young Life, we had to be with the Lord and know how to study and apply His Word, learn how to love and draw sinners to Him, be a father and mother to new "babies" in Christ, and teach growing Christians the leadership of discipleship and the humility of giving credit to others. Young Life goes beyond waiting for people to come to church and a Sunday School class. That is why I think the training we give our staff is like a graduate school in Christ. We take people who know the Lord and give them vision and tools to be effective for the Lord and in a loving, supportive, and training fellowship. This is living!

The Young Life training program is about three things:

1. To help men and women grow in their relationship with Jesus Christ.
2. To help men and women grow in their love for others
3. To help men and women learn and apply the skills of following Christ to reaching kids through the ministry of Young Life.

1. To help men and women grow in their relationship with Jesus Christ.

Just months before he died, Jim Rayburn said, at our 1970 national staff conference, "Young Life is Jesus Christ, and don't forget it... That's not just what Young Life is all about, that's *all* that Young Life's about. Young Life is just a name we use—a name we put on our brochures, our stationery, our legal papers. It means very little apart from our having a ministry with kids where we become Jesus Christ 'with skin on' to them. Kids need to see, in our lives, what we talk to them about—they need to see us walking our talk! Paul put it this way, 'For me to live is Christ.' The New Testament urges us to seek Him, to love Him, to know Him, to be committed to Him, to worship Him, to exalt Him. The Apostle says, 'Jesus Christ is all that matters.'" (Col. 3:11, PHILLIPS)

Our staff were recruited on the basis of Christ and not the benefits of Young Life. There are no benefits in Young Life that can give a person the fulfillment Jesus gives. Therefore, we talk about Jesus Christ a lot.

We talk to Him a lot. We find out why He did things, and then we do them for the same reasons. We study how He did things and seek to do them in the same way. We think about His promises and learn to trust them. We delight in applying His commandments. The Young Life Training Program is an intense focus on growing in our love and obedience to Jesus Christ.

We don't fool people. They can tell when our words drop from our teeth and do not have the deep compelling power of our life behind them. I am sure you are aware of the truth behind this statement, "We communicate in over 750 ways other than verbal." This means it is possible that we can say to one person, or 500 people, "We love Jesus Christ," and in 750 ways we are saying, "No, we don't!"

How many times have you heard speakers say basically the same things, but from some you go away changed and drawn to Christ, and from others you comment that it was a "nice talk." There is nothing so effective or powerful than a life that flows from a deep abiding relationship with Christ. The book of Acts is full of these effective people. Acts 4:13–14 describes three of them: "When they saw the courage of Peter and John and realized that they were unschooled, ordinary men, they were astonished, and they took note that these men had been with Jesus. But since they could see the man who had been healed standing there with them, there was nothing they could say." They simply had no argument with these men so changed by Christ. They were communicating far beyond words.

E. M. Bounds, in his book *Power Through Prayer*, powerfully encourages us to spend much time getting to know Christ ever more deeply. Here is one way he says it: "Can ambition that lusts after praise and precision preach the gospel of Him who made Himself of no reputation and took on the form of a servant? Can the proud, the vain, the egotistical preach the gospel full of Him who was meek and lowly? Can the bad-tempered passionate, selfish, hard, worldly man preach self-denial, tenderness?" The answer of course is a resounding "no"! Our lives built in Christ will always determine the power of our message.

I am convinced that the underlying reason why we enjoy Young Life so much is that to be effective we must be connected with Christ. Everything that is important to us and our Young Life calling is dependent on our trusting God to do it. Young Life's purpose of reaching kids for Christ presses us against Him. For example:

- What about evangelism? Can evangelism be done apart from Christ? Eph. 2:8–9 says, "For it is by Grace you have been saved, through faith—and this not from yourselves, it is the gift of God—not by works, so that no one can boast."
- What about leadership? Can we recruit and train leaders apart from Christ? Matt. 9:37–38 says, "Then he said to his disciples, 'The harvest is plentiful but the workers are few. Ask the Lord of the harvest, therefore, to send out workers into his harvest field.'"
- What about follow-up? Can we change people to be Christ-like apart from the spirit of God? Paul in 2 Cor. 3:18 says, "And we all, who with unveiled faces contemplate the Lord's glory, are being transformed into his images with ever-increasing glory, which comes from the Lord, who is the Spirit."

With all this said, my favorite fantasy of us as Young Life staff is that when we walk down the street someone might say to their friend about us, "There goes a man or woman of God." Then his friend would say, "Did you know that he/she is on Young Life staff?" The point, of course, is that we would be known first as people of God and second as "full-time Christian workers." I like to think that if Young Life quit tomorrow, you and I would keep on doing what we are doing. Jesus Christ called us and equipped us for this calling. Young Life is our method or tool.

What is the level of spiritual power in your life right now? Are people being drawn to Jesus Christ where you are? My guess is that the answer to this question is reflected in the spiritual power evident in your own life. How would you answer these questions about your own walk with Christ?

- How are you doing with Christ right now?
- Does the amount of time you spend with Him reflect your loving dependency on Him?
- How are you using and applying the Word of God?
- What is your prayer life like?
- How much do you identify with the Savior's love for the lost?
- How willing are you to lay down your life for your friends?
- Are you quick to ask forgiveness and quick to forgive?
- What is your response to Jesus when He says in John 14:15, "If you love me, keep my commands"?

These kinds of questions are the important ones in our training program. Who we are in Christ and what we are becoming in Him means everything in the effectiveness of our ministry.

2. To help men and women grow in their love for others.

In following Christ, the first thing He tells us to do is to love one another. Therefore, the atmosphere of the training program is in the context of a loving fellowship. The training program is a laboratory and helps us to learn to love people the way Christ loves. The secular world knows the power of God's love in fostering personal growth; in the book *Leadership Effectiveness* it says: "People change significantly when they have the opportunity to have a group experience and can share feelings and discuss problems in an atmosphere where they feel empathetically understood and warmly accepted." The learning environment of the training program is the fellowship of the love and acceptance of Jesus Christ.

Some of the ways we try to practice loving one another during the training are:

1. Worshipping God brings us to a humble position before one another.
2. Being quick to say we are sorry and to confess our sin builds vulnerability and openness.
3. Speaking truth and love brings freedom and growth.
4. Being quick to share feelings.
5. Desiring to learn by personal interaction.
6. Noticing and encouraging every improvement in others.
7. Being quick to compliment and give credit.
8. Performing humble acts for each other.
9. Looking for ways to serve.

3. To help men and women learn and apply the skills of following Christ in reaching kids in the ministry of Young Life.

The purpose God has called Young Life to is to reach kids for Christ and help them grow in their faith. We in Young Life are betting with our lives that sharing the gospel of Jesus Christ with kids is worth every drop of energy and commitment we have. Other people can do lots of things under the banner of Christ and must. We in Young Life have one call. We are to reach kids… all kids… for Christ. We are not the Church. We are church people doing church work, but we are pointed by our Savior towards kids. If we were a football team, we might be wide receivers, and our job would be to catch passes. If we stop catching passes or stop contributing to catching passes or just lose interest, we find another position, or we retire off the team. In Young Life, we focus the Savior's love on kids. If everyone else quits for whatever reason, we will keep going.

We are honored by Christ to have in our hands "the pearl of great price." Jesus got His energy from being with the lost. Look at His excitement when the Samaritan woman came to the well. He was exhausted… until he saw her and drew her into His redemption. In Rom. 9:1–3, Paul said he was willing to give up his own salvation in Christ if only his Jewish friends could know Christ. He hurt and longed for his people to know Christ. Do kids feel this kind of compassion coming from us? Many of us have wept over a high school as Christ wept over Jerusalem. I believe that is our call. We are the people who care enough that kids meet Christ to make it our compassionate obsession. We are on the point for the Church of Jesus Christ to gather the resources to reach kids.

I encourage each of us not to go by a school without praying for God to raise up laborers for that school or for a ministry to flourish in that school. I would like to think none of us walk by a group of kids or one kid without praying God would touch his or her heart. I like to think we on staff help focus and gather the resources of the Christian community to focus on kids. Jim Rayburn said, "There are enough Christians living around each school to reach those kids for Christ." Those of us who are called to Young Life staff are the ones called to lead the Church to kids outside their doors.

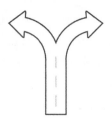

Chapter 8
WORKING WITH "BIG KIDS"

"From my years with Young Life, I thought only teenagers got excited about the Lord and responded to the Gospel. I was wrong."

When someone's good at what they do, others take notice. Young Life wasn't the only place where Chuck's many skills were recognized.

By 1974, Chuck and Linda had enjoyed five stellar years of ministry in Prince George's County. Chuck's efforts (and effectiveness) did not go unnoticed. During this time, the Reinholds attended Wallace Presbyterian Church in College Park, Maryland. They loved the pastor, Glen Knecht, who realized the man he had in Chuck and asked him to come on staff part-time with the church while still working with Young Life.

The highlight of the week for Chuck was the adult Sunday School class he began, and like so many of his previous efforts, the class quickly grew.

Meanwhile, there was growth at home, too! Linda gave birth to Chuckie in May of 1972, and Hollie followed, eighteen months later, arriving during a December blizzard. "She came into this world crying very loudly," Linda said. "The hospital nursery called her the 'crier director'! Our dear Hollie was such a welcome surprise after losing our daughter Corrie."

That year also marked a major turning point in Chuck's professional life, for that was the year he met Dr. Louis Evans, the head pastor of the National Presbyterian Church in Washington, D.C.

Nurturing the Congregation

My first impression of Dr. Louis Evans was wonderful. He was friendly and loving and showed it by his interest in me and how I was doing. I felt his sincerity. During our conversation, he asked me to come to the church and start the youth ministry.

I told him if it was just about working with the youth I would stay with Young Life. That is what Young Life is all about and there was a lot of "untouched tribes" out there.

Dr. Evans replied that he would send me to the local seminary and place me in the position of Pastor of Congregational Nurture. In this role, I would pastor adults as well as the kids.

At the time neither Linda nor I realized the magnitude of the church, but we were intrigued by Louie's offer.

(It should be pointed out that the National Presbyterian Church, in its fifty-plus year existence, has a history of ministry to many of the nation's leaders, including congressmen, senators, and presidents.)

I prayed about the possibility and in the end, gave an enthusiastic "yes." The church responded with open arms and even furnished us with a home to live in on the church grounds.

Teaching the Teacher

I would never have dreamed I would enjoy being involved full-time in a large church, but I loved it, especially because it stimulated me in my relationship with the Lord and taught me many skills in leading Bible studies and in preaching.

I began the youth ministry at the church unsure as to how these kids would respond to my Young Life style. I quickly learned kids are kids and they "long to belong." I quickly began earning the right to be heard with this new group of kids, by spending time with them so they could know me and trust me.

Our program was meeting kids outside and welcoming them as they got out of cars and again as they came through the door of our meeting room. The youth group started with a handful of kids, and it grew to over 200 within a year.

What was truly eye-opening to me, however, was the adult ministry.

After a few years, I had started a youth program, an adult Sunday School class, and the Bethel Bible series. One of the great benefits was how much I enjoyed the adult ministry. I would never have thought that. From my years with Young Life, I thought only teenagers got excited about the Lord and responded to the Gospel. I was wrong.

The adults were excited about growing in the Lord. How did I miss the fact that the Lord is "life and life abundantly" for everyone?

It was something I always knew but having to teach this "smart" adult class proved it to me. The class included top men and women in business, senators, congressmen (and common people like me). Thank you, Lord, for all of them, from the least to the greatest (and You decide which is which). I couldn't tell which was which, and I loved them all. I felt like the least, but I was sharing with them the best—our Lord and Savior and His Word!

On the surface, the adult Sunday school classes would appear to be pretty traditional in nature. There was some worship, followed by a large group teaching with small group discussion sessions. Where it differed from many other classes, however, was in application.

We never quit until everyone took something from the Bible study to apply to their lives. The Bible was not just to be read, but being God's Word, it was to be diligently applied to one's life. We asked the questions:

- What does God want us to know?
- What does God want us to feel?
- What does God want us to do?

One time, I deliberately closed the meeting *without* giving time for application, and they would not leave until we did so. We then took time for each to apply the Scripture and share it with their small group. Everyone left with a smile on their face and heart. The Lord was teaching us and changing us.

A Gift

One of the many adults the Lord was changing was Jan Augustine (Pascoe). Jan had a front row seat on my desire to not only lead the programs, but recruit spiritual, political, and community leaders to also teach the classes.

"The Bethel Bible Classes were incredible," Jan said. "Chuck convinced dozens of us to take a weekly Bible course for a year, then spend another two years teaching it! I'm SOOOO grateful for that course and the framework it gave me to understand the scope of God's plan and history. No longer did I possess just a string of Old and New Testament stories, but an understanding of how each one fit in God's plan.

"Now trusting my abilities, this framework helped me launch my own ministry teaching adults and teen Bible studies; it helped me be a

Young Life and youth group leader; it helped me take other leadership roles… and even go for my MA in Theology. I would have NEVER done any of that without that thorough and early training."

Jan also had one more accomplishment during this time. After eight months sitting under my teaching, Jan became my administrative assistant. It was no secret that organization was not my strong suit (see Pure Chuck sidebar) and Jan was truly a gift.

The Lord brought to me an amazing person: Jan Augustine Pascoe! Jan became my invaluable organizer; she understood my vision for the church. Thank you, Jan, for always enabling me to lead and reach out to my friends and staff.

PURE CHUCK (1970s)

"When I KNEW the Lord had called me to work at a church with this pastor (WHAAAT??), I tried to set up an appointment with Chuck. We had tried to meet two to three times, but he forgot each one of them and didn't show up… he could not handle his calendar! I finally wrote him a note about the date and time, watched him wad it up into the pocket of his robe, and knew he would not be there. But he was! The note was the trick—he found it the next Sunday and showed up for the meeting the next day."

—**Jan Pascoe**, Divisional Administrator,
Young Life Eastern Division

On Billy Graham, Bothering, and Bathrobes

What follows is "one of the great and wonderful memories" from my life, when I had the opportunity of spending time with Billy Graham during the spring of 1975.

We were thrilled because Billy was coming to National to give the sermon. The elders and Dr. Evans told me Billy would be very busy and should not be bothered. I knew I had to keep that in mind and keep my distance. The only problem was that no one told that to Billy! When Dr. Evans went off to pray with the choir, I was alone with Billy in the study. He immediately turned to me and asked me many questions about my life in the most loving and caring way. I told him about my involvement with Young Life. His eyes lit up and he told me how much he loved Jim Rayburn, the founder. He expressed what a man of vision and passion he was!

Dr. Evans once again expressed the need to not approach Billy as they had an important luncheon to attend. However, because he was so caring with me earlier, I boldly asked him if he could stop at our home, which was on the premises. I explained Linda had to miss church because our son was sick. Louie apologized, but said they didn't have time. Billy spoke up and said he would very much like to stop by! Mind you, this was before cell phones and as a result I could not warn Linda...

When Linda opened the front door, standing there with Dr. Evans was Billy Graham up close and personal. Here was Linda, wearing my bathrobe in front of these two great men. Chuckie was on the steps and Hollie was crying in Linda's arms. Needless to say, I was speechless! When he left our house, he gave us the warmest smile and goodbye, one I still cherish today. Billy Graham, my hero! Our Lord and Savior makes a great man very humble and lovable.

Up to this day, he remains one of the great influences on my life. I learned to look for opportunities of showing our Lord's love everywhere and all the time. Everyone is important. God loves each person. I guess that is obvious, but Billy made that truth "up close and personal" to me.

On the Home Front

When Chuckie was two, we discovered he would face unique struggles for the rest of his life. At that time his challenges were hard to diagnose, but the symptoms played out in the areas of speech and touch.

Eventually, we received more clues on what he might be encountering. Linda said, "Chuckie went to a special school for kids with severe learning problems where he could get individual affirmation. We knew he was smart, smarter than all of us.

"One doctor there told us it would be easier for Chuckie if he was blind or deaf, but his handicaps were invisible! He said Chuckie would probably relate socially to his peers by the time he was thirty. Chuckie may have had a form of autism, but back then it was almost impossible to diagnose."

In February 1976, we welcomed our newest addition to the family, Josh. By the end of the decade we had three kids under the age of five roaming the grounds of the National Presbyterian Church, and it seemed to Dr. Evans and his wife, Coke, it would be a good time for the Reinholds to move into their own house. They promised the church would help make this a reality.

"Many people came together to help us with a huge down payment," Linda said, "or it would have been impossible; even our realtor gave us his commission! In the fall of 1979 we ended up in Arlington, Virginia, with a great house that became a home for our family and many others. Josh had just turned three when we moved.

"Friends from church helped us move and prayed for the house to be blessed and used by the Lord. The first night we slept there, I remember looking out the boys' back bedroom window crying at seeing all the other homes around us. This was momentous for me, a chance to help our kids grow and have friends, be a part of a community.

"For more than thirty years we would live under that roof, experiencing everything a family can—joy, sadness, sickness, health, life, and death."

Thank You, Chuck!

What did Chuck mean to the people at the National Presbyterian Church? Their own words say it best.

Bob Hunter:

"Looking through on old 1978 calendar one day, I found this reference on October 11 of that year: 'I was born again today.' This occurred at a Chinese restaurant, where I was having lunch with Chuck. I wanted to talk to someone about my life. He was approachable and always had a smile and an encouraging word, so I called him. At that lunch I told him what a mess my life was and how I was even praying to God along the lines of 'God, I don't believe in You but if You are there, prove it by helping me.'

"I was, from the world's point of view, in great shape. I was the Federal Insurance Administrator at HUD, a position equal in rank to an Assistant Secretary. I had money. I had some fame, particularly in the insurance world. I had a wonderful wife and children. I seemed to have everything, but I was empty inside.

"When I told Chuck about my life and fumbling attempt at prayer, he showed me Revelation 3:20 and suggested my prayer had been answered since my prayer was saying 'yes' in response to Jesus' knocking. He prayed a prayer of thanksgiving and told me I should accept God was here, already in me according to His promise. This gave me a great feeling of relief and joy I could only explain as a completed transaction and I knew I was now a believer. I wept for joy into my Moo Goo Gai Pan.

"But, what did those feelings of relief and joy really mean? I did not have a clue. As I was driving back to HUD from that lunch, I knew I was a different person but how was I supposed to live? How should I act? I felt like a newborn baby, full of questions and excited to find answers.

"I met with Chuck several times a week at first and for many years at least once a week. One of the first things he did was present me with a Bible and suggest I read the four Gospels and the Book of Acts—over and over again."

Charlie Glendinning:

"In 1976, I was not doing well. Ten years earlier, at age sixteen, I had 'accepted Jesus as my Lord and Savior' at a showing of *The Restless Ones*, a movie produced on behalf of Billy Graham Crusades. I had been wrestling with the emotional confusion of my parents' divorce and felt my world, which previously had been so perfect, was now coming apart at the seams. I did the walk down to the front of the theater, met with someone in the dark who gave me workbooks to fill out and send back to somewhere in North Carolina; he prayed for me and I was on my way. Naturally, with no human contact, and the initial zeal over doing the workbooks having cooled and the fact I had started feeling better, I went back to life as usual.

"Ten years later, I found myself in the same condition of intense anxiety. What went wrong? If I really had Jesus in my heart and felt like this, maybe I had been wrong all along, and Hell was real and I was forever to be in a place where Jesus wasn't. That was the day I called the National Presbyterian Church and made an appointment to see Rev. Louis Evans.

"On the day of our meeting, Paula and I and our one-year-old son, Andy, walked into Louis' office and were told that Louis' plane had been delayed and he'd made arrangements for us to meet with the Associate Pastor, Chuck Reinhold. I didn't know Chuck, and the fact that Louis could not even see me only heightened my disappointment.

"Into Chuck's office we walked and the dam of my fears for my bleak future burst. Chuck listened and then began what was to become the beginning of my understanding that Jesus was a day-to-day, moment-by-moment relationship with the living God, who cared deeply about every thought, word, and deed; Who had promised never to leave me or forsake me; Who was, in fact, in me and far greater than he who was in the world. Chuck began teaching me, 'Without faith it is impossible to please God;' I saw for the first time 'Jesus had done it all, was alive, and wanted to begin building a relationship with me. And He was doing it through Chuck.

"My introduction to Chuck proved to be a miracle of providence and I smile now at my initial disappointment. It's to Chuck I owe my deepest thanks and eternal gratitude. He took the time and effort to help me find the lost key to the door of my heart that Jesus had been knocking on for so long; a knock I believe I could hear but couldn't find where I had left the key. I say, 'God bless him forever!' Chuck has already blessed me forever."

Robert McLeod:

"I first met Chuck in 1978 when I moved to Washington, D.C., to work in politics. The first thing I did upon my arrival was to look up the Evans family, for I had known their oldest three children, Dan, Tim, and Andie from high school in La Jolla.

Coke Evans told me about the Master's Fellowship, which was a young adult's group at the National Presbyterian Church. I had become a Christian at the age of fifteen, having had a profound revelation of the person and work of Jesus Christ through Young Life. Not knowing what to do about this new and strange reality, I lapsed into former ways, and devised newer and more sinister ways to enjoy myself and starve the Spirit within me. I attended the Master's Fellowship on what can only be described as a very trial basis, simply out of deference to the very kind yet strong urging of Mrs. Evans.

"At the very first meeting, Chuck spoke. I forget the content of what he said, but I was struck that for the first time, here was a faithful Christian and also a real man. His sense of humor, his dedication, and his winsome ways were all very attractive to a confused person like me. I also met Jan Augustine at that first meeting, who subsequently started working as Chuck's secretary. The most alarming development in this whole scenario was when I witnessed the changes in Jan's character as she spent more time with Chuck. I could only conclude that if she could do it, that is, be a successful Christian, I could as well. It was not an easy time, as I had a full schedule with girlfriend, party house, etc. Eventually, Chuck asked Jan, 'What's with this Robert guy?' He requested a lunch date, so at the appointed time I left the House Office Building where I worked, and sat on a park bench with Chuck and shared a lunch I had made. Typical of Chuck, halfway through he realized he was supposed to be fasting that day, but 'the sandwich sure was good.

"Chuck listened to my story, and said, 'Robert, you've made all the decisions you need to make. You just need to grow.' He later asked if I would move in with him and his family, as they often had young people in their home. I accepted. Breaking up with my girlfriend and announcing to my roommates that I would be leaving was the hardest decision of my life, but I knew I had to get off dead center and try out this thing I knew to be so true and, at the same time, so repulsive.

"It was as if a switch had been thrown, and as a result of my moving in with the Reinholds, I was now on the winning side, and everything hard before was now easy. The first evening Chuck drank a beer with me, and I realized all my anxiety about being a Christian was really a lie of the Devil, and I was now embarking on a life of freedom and purpose.

"I lived with the Reinholds at 5024 North 27th Street in Arlington for two years, until I left to be married to Nancy. What do I remember of that period? Many, many things, all of them good. Instead of experimenting with the content of my bloodstream, I took part in Christian ministry and instruction every night of the week. Weekends were spent fixing the cars of the young people in the Reinhold's orbit, for cost of parts only, with cars lined up and down the street each weekend. Chuck's cars needed lots of attention, as he had a Fiat and a Chrysler; nothing more need be said. Each morning I would get up to go to work, and Chuck would already be up, reading to Chuckie, making sure he was singled out, loved, and indoctrinated as a first born should be. Hollie was a cute little thing, the most innocent soul ever born. Josh was wild, all boy, on his Big Wheel, seeing how fast he could make the corner from the sidewalk into his driveway.

"Leaving the Reinholds was a big change, but I'll always consider Chuck the one person who showed me what it means to be a Christian man, and who helped me discover the unique gifts I bring to the work of the Kingdom. Before, I thought I had to become a goofy nerd with no appreciation for God's creation. Chuck showed me that when walking with Christ, there is ample room for service, fun, relaxation, discovery, challenge, and love. Soon after getting married, I made the decision to leave secular work and become an Episcopal priest and have been for thirty years now. None of this could have been possible without Chuck and Linda, who willingly opened up their home to a young man who may have had potential but was doing his best to mask it.

"When it comes to bearing fruit, fruit that lasts, the Reinholds are among the most remarkable people God has ever called as servants. I owe everything to them."

These are just three of the many people who know Christ in an intimate way, because of a loving friend by the name of Chuck.

Principles Learned Along the Way

- Meaningful time is always filled with fun and laughter. I have always felt from my Young Life days that it was God who gave us humor and laughter. I can only imagine the fun and laughter Jesus and the twelve experienced together. I can almost hear the disciples saying, "This is living!"
- My biggest and most important "take away" absolutely from this experience was this: The Word of God speaks the truth that people need, love, and desire!

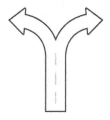

Chapter 9

BACK IN THE SADDLE AGAIN

"There is nothing more satisfying than being with a man or woman who is much with Jesus Christ. He is Life."

Throughout the Scriptures, the number seven often represents perfection or completion. It's fun to think that in the Lord's estimation, the seven years Chuck spent at the church were just the right amount too. In 1981, Young Life called again, and Chuck recognized the time was right to return to the other work he loved.

Chuck cherished those seven years at the National Presbyterian Church; in his time there he helped countless men and women come to know Jesus and grow in their walk with Him. On August 17, 1981, the church threw a celebration service for the Reinholds and the corresponding program featured this review of Chuck's tenure:

In all areas of the church can be seen the effects of our Minister of Congregational Nurture. Our adult Sunday School Program has grown each year to where there are now over 300 adults in eight classes actively involved every Sunday morning. Chuck began meeting weekly with a handful of young teenagers in a discipleship prayer group that developed into a large, active youth group, led today by other men and women he has discipled for Jesus Christ. The Bethel series began with twenty teacher trainees meeting every week and the series continues to grow as the sixteenth class begins this autumn, numbering over 450 adults involved in personal Bible study since the congregational phase began in 1977. And nineteen NPC members hold Associate in Ministry certificates from the Christian Studies Institute with many more soon completing their study.

Hitting the Ground Running

That fall I returned to Young Life staff, but this time as a regional director. The person in this role is responsible for shepherding the area directors under their supervision. At forty-two years old, I was excited to rejoin my many friends on staff and continue to point their gaze toward Jesus. It was also an opportunity for me to jump back into leading the training program, one of my favorite parts of the ministry. Fortunately, for this administratively-challenged staff man, Jan Pascoe also made the move from National Pres to continue serving as my administrator with Young Life.

As regional director, I hit the ground running and once again started a new club; this time at Arlington's Yorktown High.

"Chuck believed everyone, no matter what level of leadership they were, should run a club," Linda explained.

As my influence grew in the regional role, mission leadership decided I was ready for even more responsibility. In 1987, Doug Burleigh became

Young Life's fourth president and he appointed me to be the field vice president of the Eastern Division.

The 1980s and '90s proved to be one of Chuck's richest periods of influence; his leadership impacted the lives of so many all along the Eastern half of the U.S. (and beyond). Anyone who has spent any considerable time with the man, it seems, has a "Chuck story." Whether close to home or at a Young Life camp or a training conference, Chuck never failed to provide his friends many lessons and laughter. What follows are the firsthand accounts of men and women spurred on by Chuck and his wisdom during these golden years...

"Around Town"

"My relationship with Christ began at Saranac where Chuck and I got to be good friends, and our friendship just grew from there. Almost every Friday morning for the next two years we met together, sometimes with a couple of other guys and sometimes just us. He would come every week and pick me up, sitting in his blue Ford Escort practicing memory verses while I finished my paper route. When I opened the car door he usually said, 'Good morning glory!' He taught me how to read the Bible and pray. We talked and laughed a lot. It was a very special time. I didn't know he was a big deal in Young Life until later. He was just my friend. What stood out the most was his belief in me. He always told me he appreciated how much I loved people (so I started to love people!). We became very close and could talk about anything.

"At one leadership meeting on a Saturday morning, Chuck started our time by announcing Young Life, as an organization, was disbanding. Of course, we were all upset, and he let us talk for a while. I remember him saying how much we would miss the camps. Then he said something I will never forget. 'Now let's get back to talking about how we are going to reach these kids.' Just like that, he brought us right back to what was most important. Then, of course, he told us Young

Life was fine and he was just using that to remind us of what we were doing. It was awesome."

—**Joe Marks**, Chuck's Club kid at Yorktown in
High School from 1982–1986, and Young Life staff

"I asked Chuck to speak at my fundraising banquet and as the day drew near, I probably reminded him of the date and of the venue and thanked him vigorously. Soon enough the time came; the guests began arriving and the program needed to start. The emcee found me and whispered in my ear that Chuck hadn't arrived yet. There was never a doubt in my mind he would come; he was not one to be late, generally, but traffic in D.C. being what it can be or the parking problem at the venue presenting some challenge, he would no doubt overcome it all.

"Introductions of local luminaries were made, and the first hint of Young Life humor was introduced; the meal was served—still no Chuck. I contend to this day I wasn't worried, exactly.

"Then, as dessert was being served, Chuck strode into the room in a dapper blue suit and sat at an empty space at a table near the door. Sitting next to Chuck was one of my Young Life volunteer leaders, Eric Clausen. As I neared the table I saw Chuck bend down in his chair as if he was looking for something on the floor or tying his shoe. Eric was talking to him and holding his upper arm. When I got close enough to greet him I realized Eric was keeping him from falling off the chair. Chuck was pale as a tea cup and had put his head down to ward off a full faint. His hand was wrapped in a cloth entirely soaked in blood. The music was starting, and it was time for the program to begin with me giving a brief speech before introducing our main speaker. Fortunately, Eric had some first aid expertise associated with his livelihood. As I moved toward the podium Eric and Chuck left the main room for a handy bathroom triage center or something.

"Now, I'm not sure what to do at the podium. I was not sure our speaker was going to live, much less be able to speak to us. I began my stump speech about our local work using every word ever printed about Young Life. I quoted Jim Rayburn and used entire segments from the Time for Living camp film which had been burned into our memory after 100 showings… 'Young Life is not just a dream to remember, but a reality to live by…'

"As I neared the end, Chuck and Eric strode back into the room. Eric returned to his table and Chuck, looking like $10 million, stepped to the stage. I just had time to say his name before a great applause of welcome erupted. Gone was the great bloody rag on his hand replaced by two sterile looking, but oversized, flesh-colored band aids on two fingers. I'm not sure anyone else noticed. I backed off the stage in awe and found my seat as he started to talk about Jesus and kids and leaders and donors and staff and Jesus again and again. It was perhaps the best talk I ever heard him give. People remarked about it for weeks. And, I think we raised more money that night than ever before or since.

"Chuck was fairly mobbed as soon as the talk was done. There were many there who had been profoundly impacted by his ministry long before that night. I made a beeline for Eric. I didn't need to say anything, Eric's eyes were as big as hubcaps, and he started talking. 'Chuck chopped off most of the ends of two of his fingers,' said Eric with a flourish.

"'Did he say how?' I asked.

"'With a lawn mower,' Eric answered.

"Chuck was cutting the grass in his yard and bent down to remove a stick close to the discharge port on the lawn mower. Too close, it seems, and the mower took the tips of two fingers. Good and heroic men I have known would have called an ambulance at that point. Brave and stalwart men would have driven themselves to an emergency room. Chuck Reinhold dressed himself in a three-piece suit and drove across town to speak at a banquet. I think he did it because he didn't want to let me down. But there is a chance he didn't want to pass up the opportunity to talk about Jesus and it had nothing to do with me.

"Imagine Linda's surprise when she arrived home and found the blood-stained bandages in Chuck's bathroom used to treat the initial injury—lots of bandages and tee shirts and probably towels, but no Chuck. Eric was in for a pound now and drove Chuck straight to the hospital where they did what they could for him until a surgeon could be arranged to do skin grafts the next morning.

"I've never stopped backing away in awe of this man of God. I'm only a little surprised he didn't pick up the two severed fingertip pads from the newly cut grass and miraculously re-attach them."

—**Mike O'Leary**, Young Life President, Canada

"In Conference"

"Chuck once asked our training group, 'When you are in a room full of people, where would you want to sit if what the speaker was saying was of critical importance to you, such that you didn't want to miss a word?' We looked at each other and realized we had to say it would be in the front. Then he asked, 'What would be the most important topic in the world?' We knew this required a Sunday School answer: Jesus. 'So,' he continued, 'if someone were speaking about Jesus where would you want to sit?'

"At that Williamsburg conference our training group was observed to rush to the front of the room and fight with each other over the seats closest to the podium! We did the same thing at the next session of Young Life Institute and got the same quizzical response. I still sit up front if I think the topic is important."

—**Ethel Burwell Dowling**, Former Young Life staff

"One time, a seminar leader cracked a joke about bald people and Chuck was the focal point of the joke. After people sheepishly laughed, Chuck leaned over to me and said, 'That guy just lost points with everyone in the room by making fun of me—they're just glad it isn't them.' And he was SO right... It burned into my brain that getting a laugh at other people's expense is a cheap way to gain affirmation and not to do it. The great part was Chuck also thought the joke was funny, but not when it comes at someone's expense."

—**Pat Goodman**, Forty-year Young Life staff, who met Christ when Chuck spoke on a Hilltop Ranch weekend

---

PURE CHUCK (circa 1990s)

"Pat Goodman told the story about a time Chuck drove up from Virginia to Baltimore to see him. When Chuck arrived, Pat saw Chuck had his emergency brake on (and had it on the entire trip from Virginia). Pat asked if he always drives with the emergency brake on. Chuck doesn't flinch. He doesn't look at Pat. He just said, 'Sometimes I do... and sometimes I don't.' (I think he kept the brake on.)"

—**Andy Fetzer**, Young Life staff

"The 90-Day Challenge: At one of our monthly staff meetings, Chuck challenged us all to ninety straight days of having a consistent 'quiet time.' Tomorrow would be day 'one.' If we missed a day, we had to start all over. It did not matter if it was day 'twenty-one' or day 'eighty-nine,' it was back to day 'one' and the start of a new ninety days. I left there like all leaders who enjoy a good challenge, invigorated, and ready to go.

"Easier said than done. Ninety days came and went, no one had made it yet. I was struggling so much I began to secretly hope Chuck had forgotten the challenge. Part of my issue was deciding what 'counted.' If I quickly read some verses before I went to bed, even if it was after midnight, was that legit? What if I prepared a lesson for Campaigners, did this count as my personal time with God? Who was I fooling? There were just plenty of days I missed.

"Then it happened. Months later we were again gathered as a staff, and Chuck announced the first person had completed their ninety days. Without his saying the name of the person, I knew immediately who it was. In those years, I worked alongside Mike O'Leary in Prince George's County, Maryland. Mike and I met weekly to plan. Mike's suggestions and input were becoming better and better. As an idea person, I was used to making a significant contribution. But my thoughts were paling in contrast to Mike's insight. In the moment Chuck announced someone was done, it was crystal clear to me. Mike was positioning himself to hear from God, and I saw a living demonstration of what could happen when God had that kind of access. Sure enough, it was Mike. And sure enough, I did ninety in a row starting the next day. It was no longer a challenge, it was a way of life I wanted for myself."

—**Sue Cryer Moye**, Young Life staff, 1981–1988

"Perhaps it was a Campaigner meeting or weekend camp seminar. Chuck was giving a talk from the Scriptures and I'm pretty sure there was a chalkboard. Suddenly, he looked right at me and stopped his talk. He inched a little closer, bending toward me, and in a more personal tone but still loud enough for everyone in the room to hear, he said, 'Mike, how long do you expect to be a Christian?'

"A personal eternity passed as I tried to discern if it was a rhetorical question but not wanting to risk it, I said, 'A long time, Chuck.'

"Then he said, 'Well then, don't you think you ought to be taking some notes?'

"I still live in fear when I attend a sermon, seminar, or PTA meeting that the speaker will look at me and ask me the same question, so I always at least pretend to take notes."

—**Mike O'Leary**

"Camp Stories"

"In 1985, I'd just graduated from college with a double major in 'I don't want to do this for the rest of my life' and 'I have no idea what to do with the rest of my life.' Those four years had been riddled with a pursuit of identity and small steps to grow the mustard seed of faith planted in high school.

"When I arrived at Geneva College I was hungry for something; I just had no idea what it was. Over those four years, I helped build a new club, pulled together a team of leaders, took kids to camp, led a few people to Jesus, and learned some veiled things about leadership. The truth is, I never saw myself as a leader; I needed to be told. The man who told me was Chuck.

"That summer following college graduation I went on a short-term mission trip to Haiti. I came back with clarity that I was called to something, I just didn't know what! There was talk from my dad about an offer from Niagara Mohawk, our local utility company. My dad worked there, and I was hired the past several summers to paint electrical structures. It was scary but paid well and had a sense of adventure to it. For a kid growing up with very limited resources, a job at Niagara Mohawk was a ticket to security and a consistent paycheck. My divorced parents loved the idea of me having this level of security and income. As a family, we grew up on public assistance and a secure job meant everything. After Haiti, I served as a cook at Windy Gap. That's where I met Chuck.

"Chuck was the speaker—fun, full of life and wisdom. Growing up in a single parent home that lacked most of what Chuck embodied, listening to him speak and talking with him was water on parched ground. What some may have experienced after college with their dads talking and dreaming about life and what was ahead, I experienced with Chuck.

"Within the first week I asked Chuck if we could connect and talk about life. Mostly I wanted to talk about my life and what to do with it. Growing up, I had a distant relationship with my father; this left me wanting for input and direction in my life from someone I could respect. Chuck was an answer to a prayer I did not have the wisdom to pray. In Romans, it talks about the Spirit interceding on our behalf in ways we do not know or understand. Prayers we do not have the wisdom yet to pray, God often answers with people and His person in my life was (and continues to be) Chuck.

"I remember what it felt like when Chuck walked into the summer staff housing and asked people where I was. 'Do you know Rick Rogan? Can you find him and tell him I'm looking for him?' I'll never forget that. Looking back, I realize it was Chuck mirroring Jesus, stepping into people's lives, looking for them, taking initiative, and calling them by name. That month, Chuck sought me out and we'd talk about Jesus and life. I remember the questions Chuck asked:

"'When in your life did you sense the presence of Christ the strongest?'

"'When did you pray the most?'

"'What brought you the most joy or fulfillment in the past three years?'

"Then he'd ask what I was learning from my times in the Word. I shared that in high school I depended on the opening half hour of my day to read and journal the Gospels just to survive and stay connected to the love of God in Christ. For Chuck, if this was an interview, I was hired. Chuck loves Scripture and that's where we connected! When Chuck talked about Scripture and what he was learning, it energized me and engaged my heart. At the time I was reading in the gospel of Luke and praying God would reveal His will for my life.

"Over the last week of our time at Windy Gap, Chuck encouraged me to go on Young Life staff. He remembered our previous conversations and reminded me of what the Lord was saying. He asked for two years and told me it was like a graduate school for Christ. I remember his passion, 'You don't go to grad school and ask, "How much am I going to get paid?" You go to learn, and, in this case, you will be growing in Christ and learning stuff that will prepare you for the rest of your life!'

"That's what Chuck does best, speaks into lives with the wisdom and voice of Jesus. He was affirming and challenging, gracious and convicting, and all along the way pushed me toward Jesus and Scripture. Chuck did not talk about career; he talked about a calling. He asked about my fears and what was holding me back. Chuck spoke to me in a way that brought life and created vision, where I was empty and had none. I never had anyone speak to me in a way that communicates such a belief or a confidence available in Christ.

"His words and encouragement were always one step ahead of who we really were at that moment. Wanting those encouragements to become true, we'd then follow Chuck as he followed Christ. That's how Chuck led us.

"In my four years in high school, our area went through four different Young Life staff people. Each left because there was never enough financial support. Growing up the way we did, I did not want my faith tested financially. In one of my final conversations with Chuck at camp, I committed to moving back to Tonawanda, New York, working for Niagara Mohawk, giving money to Young Life, and starting a Young Life club as a volunteer.

"Chuck settled for that answer but also said he'd pray for me and ask the Lord to speak to me about my calling. At that time in my Bible I wrote Windy Gap July/1985 next to Luke 12:47: 'That servant who knows his master's will and does not get ready or does not do what his master wants will be beaten with many blows.' A soul outside the will of God is truly a beaten soul.

"I drove away from Windy Gap with a battle raging in my soul. It was God's call in Chuck's voice and Luke 12 painted the battle lines: value, security, money, provision, calling, and leaving home. The 'do not worry' statements in that chapter were a list of my fears. Chuck was right—the Word of God will speak to us. Chuck told me we read and hear the Word of God differently when we're called. We read it differently because when we're called we have to risk, and when we risk we really need God's Word and promises to be true.

"I offered to drive someone else from Windy Gap to another Young Life camp called Southwind in Florida. After leaving Southwind, I continued to drive south, still praying and battling this calling the Lord had put on my life. I pulled off at a random exit to get a cup of coffee and pray. I sat alone praying and asking God to speak and for a small sign about what to do with my life. Then Chuck walked in! He looked as if he may be lost, and he probably was, but God used Chuck to find me.

"I laughed out loud! Chuck walked over and sat down. 'I drove and followed you all the way down here to ask you again to go on staff.' I knew he was lying. (I'm pretty sure Linda was driving because Chuck's an awful driver.) Then my soul laughed; the battle was over. Chuck was and continues to be a voice calling me and others to Christ.

"That was in July 1985. I've been on Young Life staff for thirty-three years. On my Young Life application, I said I planned on being on staff for two years, just as Chuck asked. Over each of the past thirty-three years, the Lord has used the voice of Chuck Reinhold to speak into my life. Although the conversations are fewer and may take place virtually, the significance and depth of impact have the same eternal results."

—Rick Rogan

"I called Chuck because our son Greg was having an extremely difficult time. This is who Chuck is: he said, 'Hey, I know the perfect thing for him. Send him to Saranac. This is my month off at Saranac but I'm going to tell them I'm going to go up and be work crew boss and take charge of Greg.' The job was to dig latrine ditches, but Chuck went out and did it with him all month. Greg thought the world of Chuck and still does thirty years later. That was the experience of a lifetime and cemented in my son's heart and mind the importance of personally knowing the Lord. He would say it was the summer of his life as far as his Christian faith goes. Chuck exemplified the message of 'live the gospel and occasionally use words.'"

—Bill Malarkey, Lifelong friend

"In July of 1986, I was leading kids from Connecticut at Saranac. I somehow injured my back and was unable to go on the hike up Mt. Ampersand. As I saw the kids and other leaders off, Chuck asked, 'Tony, you're not going on the hike today, right?'

"'Yes, that's right. Just going to rest.'

"'Well, since you're just kind of hanging around today, maybe you could write us a new song for club. A song that talks about the amazing love of Christ and how it is always with us.'

"'Okay, I'll give it a try but sometimes songs can happen quickly, or they can take days, weeks, months, or even years to be completed.'

"'Yes, that's true, but it's going to be really quiet here today so why don't you get your guitar and some paper and head to the lake and take some time to pray about the song and see what God will do.'

"'Okay, Chuck, I'll do that, and we'll see what God will do.'

"I grabbed my guitar, a pen, and a couple of paper placemats and went down to the waterfront to pray and 'see what God might do.' *It's Amazing* was written in a couple of hours in the quiet and beauty of the waterfront at Saranac.

"When Chuck returned, we went into the counselor's lounge and I started to share the song. I got through the first verse and chorus and Chuck ran out to get more people to listen. So, I started the song again and again. I got partway through and Chuck ran out and got more people to listen along including the program directors. This time I got all the way through the song and I could see by the smiles on everyone's faces the song was good. Chuck was smiling the biggest and said, 'The chorus will be like an anthem for kids everywhere to rally around and know that God has always loved them all the time, everywhere.'

"That night we introduced the song and sang it every night until camp was over. Chuck was the instrument by which God moved me to write a song that's touched thousands of lives in all parts of the world. *It's Amazing* has been translated into many different languages and after thirty years is still a favorite at Christian summer camps, Young Life clubs, and churches around the world."

—**Tony Congi**, Musician and former Young Life staff

It's Amazing

[Chorus]
It's amazing how You love me
It's amazing how You care
It's amazing how You're always thinking of me
All the time—everywhere.

[Verses]

I have searched the whole world over

Looking for the things

That I thought would fill my heart and ease my pain.

I can climb the highest mountain or sail beyond the seas

And it always brings me back to You again...[Chorus]

There are times when I feel lonely

I'm twisted up inside

On who I am and what I want to be.

There's a yearning deep inside of me

And a longing to be free

And it always brings me back to You again...[Chorus]

[Bridge]

Well, I have lived my life an outlaw on the run

Leavin' broken-hearted dreams for everyone.

No matter what I do

No matter what I've done

It always brings me back to You again...

I can look the whole world over thinkin' that I'll find

Another one who'll know me like You do

No matter where I go

No matter where I've been

It always brings me back to You again... [Chorus]

Principles Learned Along the Way

"One of my favorite lines from Chuck came while we were on Assignment at Saranac in 1990. I followed him around all month and learned how to encourage and disciple others. It was a great joy and blessing for me in my first year on staff. During that time, I heard Chuck say to people, 'You will be great for God when being great is not your god.' What a gift to hear this so early in ministry and life. We are called to humility and service. It has shaped much of who I am and how I train others."

—**Mike Cramer**, Young Life staff

"At one leadership meeting, we were in the room waiting to start and it was 5:03. Leadership started at 5pm. Chuck grabbed me and said 'Pete, what time does this meeting start? Why are we starting late?' He went on to explain we should always start on time and value everyone's time. And now I always start a meeting on time!"

—**Pete Hardesty**, Young Life staff

"Chuck and I were walking across Atlantic Avenue in Virginia Beach during a staff intern training time and I was sharing with him how much pressure I was feeling to get a great club going at Monacan High School in Richmond, and how I wanted to build a great area for the Lord. Chuck stopped me in my tracks with this statement, 'You only need to do two things in Richmond this year—grow in Christ and learn.' I have never forgotten this sage advice and I quote it often. It freed me up to focus on what was important—Jesus and learning from Him, two things I have continued to focus on thirty-five years later, still on Young Life staff!"

—**Casey Dunn**, Young Life staff

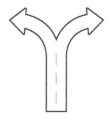

Chapter 10
A PRINCIPLED MAN
By Mike O'Leary

W hen Chuck became the vice president of the Eastern Division, he had a group of us he would ask for advice and try things out on. He understood the power of leadership with a unique clarity and those of us in the little group realized we were on holy ground. There was plenty of discussion, even disagreement, before an idea or a principle "went public" but we all understood once it was "out there" we needed to be all in.

In this case, Chuck saw a few things that were problems in the leadership community at the time. He wanted to set three divisional principles that would become our becoming. The first was simple and didn't need to be stated to address a problem, but I remember Chuck had asked a staff person about his "quiet time" and the poor, somewhat innocent, soul had sighed and said, "I'm so busy, I just don't have time." Thus, was born the first divisional principle:

1. NOTHING IS MORE IMPORTANT THAN YOUR RELATIONSHIP WITH CHRIST!

When Chuck spoke on his divisional principles, which he was eventually asked to do all around the mission, he would spend nine-tenths of his time on this principle. It was by far his favorite, and there was never any doubt about this one.

The second principle was born out of a leadership perspective he had that there was way too much competition between staff regarding the size and progress of their areas. Numbers of summer campers and of volunteer leaders were a currency among the staff at one point. One of the problems was our growth in summer camping was being squeezed by a limited number of spots at Saranac and Windy Gap. I'm not sure when Lake Champion entered the picture, but when it first did, it was not the soup du jour. Summer camp quota meetings were a deadly game of survival of the fittest. The right dates and number of spots were critical to success, at least in our small minds. So, Chuck found a principle that would address this. And this is where the brilliance of setting a new bar—having a vision for people to grow into—collided with "it's a hard habit to break."

2. YOUR AREA (REGION, CLUB, CAMP TRIP, WORK CREW SPOT) IS MORE IMPORTANT THAN MINE!

Staff wrestled with this one. Some tried to point out the inherent circular argument. If two people discuss limited resources and both strictly maintain, "Your area is more important than my area," then no one can blink. If I say, "You take the choice camp spots, your area is more important than mine," then the other area director has to say, "No, you take them, your area is more important than mine." But somehow, the division never got stuck in an endless loop. It was pretty clear in our conscience what this meant to us and for us. The idea of "fighting" for kids and leaders in my area against staff who were fighting back for kids and leaders in their area had to give way to a sense of synergy. There were obviously very strong areas as well as those who needed help to find their strength. This principle meant strong area directors got stronger in the Kingdom of God and the cause of Christ by giving the weaker areas what they could to help them grow. It was not a line, a quote, or a law you ever said to anyone else. But, you knew in your heart and we knew in the community who was being true to this principle and those folks became better leaders.

The third principle developed in the same cauldron as the second and for some of the same reasons. Summer camp spots were painfully limited in a time of exponential grow in the numbers of clubs and kids across the division. There was genuine angst about it because we had all been bred to fill our buses and work tirelessly to get kids to camp so they could meet Jesus on the point at Saranac or by the pool at Windy Gap or on Mt. Princeton at Frontier Ranch. Chuck felt this angst and he didn't want to diminish the passion, but there was no other solution than to address the core of the problem. If we could not get more spots for kids to go to camp to meet Jesus, then:

3. KIDS WILL MEET CHRIST IN THE LOCAL AREA!

Certainly, having twenty minutes of silence at camp to consider the powerful talk they'd just heard about the cross of Christ was a gift to kids. Looking out at the beauty of God's creation inspired them to reflect on the immensity of God and His personality and love for them. But… what was to stop us from inviting kids to give their lives to Christ in the parking lot of the local high school if we had earned the right, if we had preached Christ in everything we did with them, and if we had cared for them as the Savior did?

Well, one of the things stopping us was we didn't know exactly how to do it face-to-face. We had become comfortable having a speaker do it in a crowd… and often learning about a kid's response in the Say-So the next day. We needed to learn how to invite kids personally, which meant learning the Navigator's Bridge illustration—twelve verses explaining the Gospel and the way to knock, seek, and find peace with God. Or, just have a copy of Campus Crusade's Four Spiritual Laws, "Do you know God loves you and has a wonderful plan for your life?" This principle demanded we become fluent in the Gospel message and practice the courage to invite kids personally in our home courts.

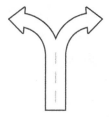

Chapter 11

ETHIOPIA:
THE SEQUEL

"It is the greatest privilege I can think of to go to the poorest country in the world and give kids the unsurpassed and unsearchable riches of Jesus Christ, the 'pearl of great price.'"

It's a special gift when the Lord calls us to return to a place that's meant so much to us in our lives. When Chuck reached his fifty-ninth birthday in 1998, he was preparing for his next grand adventure. By this point, Young Life's "minister at large" had served on Young Life staff for almost thirty years. Those three decades of ministry, along with the seven spent at the National Presbyterian Church, can trace their humble beginnings to the year he spent as a young college graduate serving overseas.

Testing the Waters

Throughout the years, Ethiopia never left my heart. I returned to the country four more times, three with Linda. Most notable among these visits was the sabbatical I enjoyed there in 1972. It was then I met Abraham Fiseha, a high school kid running around town.

While in Ethiopia, Linda and I invited Abraham to live with us, and he began his own journey with Jesus Christ. From 1972 through 1993, Abraham lived in the U. S. and Canada, studying and ministering. After twenty-one years away, Abraham and his family returned to Ethiopia, where his work with Hope International endeared him to many of the highest political, business, and religious leaders in the country.

Abraham and I discussed the possibility of beginning youth ministry in Ethiopia and in the fall of 1997, at Abraham's invitation, I went to Addis Ababa to speak at an all-day youth rally sponsored by the International Evangelical Church called "Shout for Joy." The leadership team put up a few posters around the city advertising the event and eagerly expected they might have fifty kids show up.

By 9:00 on the morning of the rally, more than 1,000 kids were waiting to come in; they stayed the whole day and loved it.

The day before the rally, the church hosted a "Youth Leaders Seminar," where they anticipated ten to twenty-five potential leaders might attend. To their surprise, ninety men and women came out to the day-long seminar, many of whom had jobs but skipped work that day to learn how to care for kids.

These two events spoke volumes to the leadership of Young Life, which encouraged me to further pursue the idea of starting ministry there. I was still motivated by the phrase "kids furthest out," the kids without our Lord and Savior. It didn't take me long to figure out where that next place would be. It was Ethiopia, the place where I first felt the call to go to the untouched tribe of kids in high schools. Wow, what a challenging call, but it was the one I was looking for.

And I wasn't alone.

"I knew this day would come," Linda said. "Since first meeting Chuck, I knew of his love for Ethiopia! I was ready, willing, and able."

In a letter to our many financial and prayer supporters, I outlined the reasons I believed God was calling me back:

1. Ethiopia is the oldest continuous Christian country in the world.

2. Ethiopia is the poorest country in the world (*USA Today*).

3. Think about this: 70 percent of the people are under eighteen, and 50 percent are under fifteen years of age. This is a call for Young Life to help.

4. There are no trained youth leaders in the Ethiopian church. The thrust of my ministry for the last thirty-five years has been in training men and women for the youth ministry. This makes the call to help very personal.

5. God called me to Young Life when I was in Ethiopia the first year out of college… God keeps Ethiopia on our hearts. We have an understanding and love for the people. Linda and I are an obvious choice.

6. Our friend, Abraham Fiseha, has been a friend and partner in Christ for over twenty-five years… He is now a senior elder at the International Evangelical Church in Addis Ababa, and he is huge for Christ in that great city. He will act as our partner, negotiator, and coordinator.

7. Denny Rydberg [then president of Young Life] is excited about this ministry to Ethiopia. It is an important affirmation of Young Life's purpose to "go to every kid."

8. Ethiopia is a spectacular place to train staff. Kids and potential leaders are available every day for large chunks of time. School for most is either morning or afternoon and most do not have

jobs. Their culture is much like the one Jesus walked in. Our leaders can just hang out with kids most of a day like Jesus did with His disciples.

9. I can attest to the day and night difference Jesus Christ makes in a life. I am forever grateful for Young Life not quitting before they got to me. It is the greatest privilege I can think of to go to the poorest country in the world and give kids the unsurpassed and unsearchable riches of Jesus Christ, the "pearl of great price."

Back to the Beginning

For me, the ultimate objective in returning to Ethiopia was simple. God willing, in two years we would leave behind twenty-four trained youth leaders. Think about the incredible difference twenty-four trained youth leaders would make in a country of fifty-three million. They, as well as those they touched, would multiply through the years until every school, neighborhood, business, and government office would be infiltrated with the aroma of Jesus Christ.

The plan was to bring along four leaders from the U.S. to help train the Ethiopian leaders. In October 1998, twenty-four Ethiopian men and women were selected for the inaugural training program. I met daily with the four leaders for training and supervision. Meanwhile, the four leaders each trained six Ethiopians in incarnational youth ministry. By the end of the first year, six of the twenty-four Ethiopians were chosen to help with the training of new leaders.

In 1998, taking a year off from college, our son Josh also joined in the endeavor—a literal Godsend to us, as we missed all three of our children while we were away. It also proved to be a Godsend to Josh, as he met Yodit, one of the first Ethiopian Young Life staff.

"It was love at first sight," Josh said, and the two married in 2004.

The team stayed in a compound located in Kore, one of the poorest and most dangerous areas of Addis Ababa. The compound was surrounded by a huge wall, with guards at the front gate. "When we did venture out in someone's car, it was sad," Linda said. "It was like riding through a game park watching all the people but not interacting. It killed me to ignore them, especially the children.

In the midst of this darkness, however, hope was coming. Linda, the U.S. leaders, and I spent many hours in prayer and began meeting the potential Ethiopian leaders. They eagerly came to our home in the compound, where the entire group worshipped and listened as I cast the vision for Young Life in Ethiopia.

The leaders demonstrated a great determination in attending the meetings; they had to travel long distances to get to the compound, and once there, face the guards at the gate. "We learned quickly," Linda said, "that having large groups of Ethiopians come to our compound was not usual or necessarily welcome. The guards learned their names quickly and, eventually, even they joined us!"

On the home-front, Linda quickly learned the importance of hiring as many locals as possible to give them much-needed jobs. "I found an amazing woman, Yalemwork, to be our cook and another woman to do the laundry and cleaning; Abraham found Ephrem, a wonderful driver for us. My job was to manage and care for the workers. Having never had a maid or any help before, this took a while for me to adjust to." The workers, especially Yalemwork, who served in the house during our whole time abroad, became like family to Linda and me, and as we ministered to them, they ministered right back.

It wasn't long before I was ready to start meeting kids. Taking the other leaders with me, I walked the dirt roads getting to know all kinds of young people—tough ones, shy ones, the interested and disinterested, all in the hopes of building friendships.

I put the challenging work into perspective. Was it difficult? We didn't look like them or speak their language! No, it was not. I learned quickly that friendship with the love of Jesus' Gospel was so wonderful, a message that kids were drawn to Him!

In 1999, when the time to start a Young Life club had arrived, I knew exactly what to do.

"He was so bold, brave, and had such vision," Linda said. "Before we knew it, he had gained permission to use the compound library for club. This was no small feat. Traditionally, there was a giant line separating the missionaries from the people, especially where they lived. Chuck met this criticism and hurdles time and time again."

More than fifty kids turned out to the first club.

"It was pure pandemonium but a great success!" Linda said. "We had a typical club with songs, skits, and a club talk through an interpreter. Club quickly grew to over one hundred kids."

The Shoeshine Boys

On one of my daily ventures outside the compound gate, I encountered a group of kids trying to make money in a pretty unprofitable venture: shining shoes. Immediately drawn to them, I went outside the gate to play with them day after day. Just like their counterparts in the states, these boys were drawn to me as well. While an interpreter was needed to bypass the barriers of language, the kids had no problem understanding my love for them.

Over time, I began leading a Bible study with the boys.

"They were studying the leper Jesus touched and healed," Linda explained. "Chuck asked them if they would have first touched the leper before healing him. He wasn't ready for their answer. Each one of them had parents who were lepers.

"Suddenly, the conversation got personal and Jesus became real! Not only were their parents lepers, but beggars as well. They would get up before dawn and walk miles to the city. Hundreds of these families made this trek each day, walking early in the cold, wrapped in their white gabis (chiffon shawls) going to their special place to beg! The kids, however, did not; they went to school and shined shoes."

I continued having Bible studies with the "shoeshine boys," started a soccer team with them and, eventually, found a way to send them to a boarding school outside the city.

"Can you imagine?" Linda marveled. "They had a bed, blankets, three great meals a day, friends, and school! They quickly gained weight, grew in stature and, most importantly, began to have hope and a vision for their lives."

Eight out of the nine boys graduated and went on to university. These former shoe shiners now possessed the skills necessary to obtain full-time jobs.

"This had a trickledown effect by giving a new life to each family and their surrounding neighborhoods," Linda said. "The ministry in Kore exploded and grew to over 200 kids."

The Golden Girls

While the guys and I were befriending the shoeshine boys, Linda, accompanied by Tsigereda, her guide and interpreter, went out to meet girls. "Women in general, and especially young women in Africa, have very little help in achieving any of their dreams," Linda explained. "These girls were among the poorest and most severely vulnerable."

Young Life club provided them with a safe place where they could laugh, sing, and have fun, a welcome respite from the harsh circumstances they endured daily. Linda recounted the story of another teen she encountered:

"Martha first showed up at the compound gate wrapped in a cotton shawl that looked like a burial cloth. She was so sick, weak, hungry, and cold; her eyes were scared and empty. Through an interpreter, she shared that she came from the refugee camp, lived with her mother, and had AIDS. She'd heard of our work with Young Life and hoped she would find help.

"My heart could not send her away with nothing, so we gave her some clothing and food. She returned later, but even weaker. This time we took her to the clinic and they hospitalized her for a week. She seemed to gain more strength and her eyes were showing life and hope.

"The other girls loved on her and welcomed her into the group. She'd been gripped with fear; her mom had practiced witchcraft on her. As the girls continued caring for her, she came to know the love of the Lord and was saved. Her face changed, she had laughter in her eyes, even joy. Martha died that next October, surrounded by her friends. She left this place knowing she was valuable and precious to many. She's now in the Lord's presence, free from pain and fear, waiting for us to come. Martha was a treasure who taught me so much."

During this time, Martha and the other young ladies going through similar hardships became known affectionately as the "Golden Girls."

"The name stands for young women of great value," Linda explained. "Gold is a precious commodity in Ethiopia, highly prized and appreciated. We wanted these girls to know they have tremendous value and worth. The purpose was to minister to young girls who were pregnant, already mothers, or HIV positive. We promoted self-worth by providing Bible study, prayer, English lessons, cooking and nutrition lessons, financial management skills, counseling, and training in handicrafts, (embroidery, weaving, sewing, card making, cooking). The girls earned a salary for their work and, more importantly, they gained self-respect and hope. By caring for them, we extended their lives.

The most exciting development, Linda said, came when the first group of Golden Girls assumed the leadership and vision for other unreached young women in the city. "The need was so great; we could have had four more compounds around the city and still have need for more."

Linda and the Golden Girls, and their kids.

Expansion!

In my mind, the most important part of our time in Addis Ababa was the training program with the Ethiopian staff. This time was vital to our ultimate goal of leaving the work in the hands of the Ethiopians.

"The training program was a sacred time for Chuck and became such a special experience for our staff," Linda said. "He ran it like he had his whole life! First, he communicated the importance of being on time. This was no easy feat, as the staff came from all over the city relying on unreliable public transportation. They had to take buses, taxis, and walk many miles just to get to the compound. However, they learned rather quickly, arriving early meant time for coffee and cookies from Yalemwork.

The Ethiopians soaked up what all the training program participants had before them: the basics of ministry I held so dear: the importance of Bible study, memorizing Scripture, going to where the kids were, giving club talks and Campaigner lessons, and even the Dale Carnegie principles I'd learned three decades earlier.

"Mostly," Linda said, "he challenged them to love each other with forgiveness and encouragement. They looked for ways to help each other with the thought that the other clubs were more important than their own. They loved sharing about their ministries, about the kids they were loving. Individual clubs grew in number all over the city. The staff spread out all over the city, meeting kids, having clubs and Campaigners!"

The Ethiopian staff.

PURE CHUCK (circa 2000s)

"One day there was a plan to have all the staff sleep over, have dinner, and watch a movie together. Whenever I met

Chuck on the porch or outside or in the living room, he kept on telling me how popular the movie is in the states, how romantic and funny it is, this and that.

"I was so eager to watch it… then the time for the movie came. I had Ermius and Shewan next to me. They started screaming and I started screaming and I wasn't able to stop screaming. I was waiting and expecting the romantic comedy movie. The movie was 'Psycho.'

"I think Chuck and the guys chose me for a victim that day. Later on, I liked the whole plan."

—**Alemtsehay Sahle**, Ethiopian Young Life staff

Kids came from all faith backgrounds: Orthodox, Muslim, Evangelical, and even no faith at all. Fearful of the large groups gathering in one spot, the government sometimes cracked down on the leaders; one time arresting three of the staff. They were undaunted, however.

"We began having all-city clubs and over 600 kids would come," Linda smiled. "It was amazing to hear club kids give their testimonies and the singing was awesome! The kids always listened with great appreciation to the message."

"Chuck's vision had come to fruition," Linda exclaimed. "The seed planted so long ago during his first time in Ethiopia was now a reality! Of course, none of this was possible without the myriads of friends and supporters from the states. They saw Chuck's heart and stepped up to enable and empower him. Today, Ethiopia Young Life is led by Moges Berassa and a shining example to all of Africa!" And, most recently, Moges has begun a club in Gambella where Chuck first went in 1961 out of love and respect for Chuck.

Young Life in Ethiopia is indeed going strong. Consider this encouraging report:

Currently, Young Life is active in schools and neighborhoods throughout Addis Ababa and in twenty-four different town and villages around Ethiopia. Over the last seven years, Young Life in Ethiopia has grown 34 percent per year and currently over 15,000 kids attend Young Life outreach clubs every week and almost 7,000 kids are involved in weekly discipleship groups. Over 7,000 kids and leaders will attend outreach and discipleship camps with Young Life in Ethiopia this summer. (From the Young Life Ethiopia website, December 2017)

Indescribable Loss

By 2005, the original plan of spending two years in Ethiopia had stretched out past seven! Linda and I were more than happy to remain there until we received the news no parent is ever prepared to hear: Chuckie had been diagnosed with cancer.

That was a life-changer for sure. We went back to the United States to be with him and get him the proper treatment. It was hard to leave Ethiopia, but we were happy to do it for Chuckie.

"Chuck and I left with such mixed emotions," Linda acknowledged, "but we knew Young Life Ethiopia would continue, even thrive because of the staff."

Arriving back in Virginia, we sought a second opinion on Chuckie's health, but the doctor agreed with the original diagnosis. Tragically, the news grew worse, as he told us the cancer was incurable and Chuckie did not have long to live.

We were devastated. I've never felt more sad or depressed, but we still trusted the Lord for His very best.

On September 23, 2007, Chuckie entered the arms of his beloved Savior. He was now pain-free and in the glorious presence of Jesus, whom he loved so well while on this earth.

Josh remembered the emotion of these days. "My brother had just died, and I still have the picture in my head of the expression on his face when his spirit left his body. Surrounding his bed, as a family, we listened to praise music and let him know how loved he was as he took his final breaths. That was one of the most traumatic moments of my life.

"When the funeral home gave us one last opportunity to see Chuckie, my father and I walked into a very dimly lit room with my brother lying on a table; he now looked at peace. As we stood there, my father began to weep over my brother's body. I had never seen my father cry like that, so this was big to me. I saw how devastating the loss of his oldest son was for him. I didn't know how to react, so I just turned and hugged him.

"My father could stick his hand in a lawn mower, wrap it in a paper towel, drive forty-five minutes and speak at a Young Life banquet without showing much emotion, but this was too much for him. I feel blessed to have shared this moment with my dad. It was beyond devastating, but I was there to truly see his feelings."

The entire Reinhold family gathered at Hollie's home in Nashville to celebrate Chuckie's thirty-fifth birthday. This photo was taken over that birthday weekend. Chuckie went to be with Jesus a few months later.

Over 500 people came to Chuckie's memorial service, many out of respect to our family, but mostly for their love of their friend, Chuckie. Years later, I could share this testimony, "We're thankful to the Lord for Chuckie's life and God's purposes. I knew he was with his sister, Corrie, my mom and soooo many wonderful people, and most of all, our loving, wonderful Lord and Savior, Jesus Christ. I miss him terribly, but I'm not sad for him. I know he's happier than he's ever been, and I know my mom and dad were excited to see him. And I know we'll see him again. After that experience, I can honestly say I have no fear of death. I just want to live my life for the praise of Jesus Christ's glory... seriously!"

Principles Learned Along the Way

From Ethiopian leaders:

"One of the first questions Chuck always asked me when we would get together was, 'How are you doing in the Lord?' I couldn't help but want to get to know the Lord more and more. My faith was strengthened every day. One of the most remarkable aspects of Chuck's ministry in Ethiopia was the fact that he wanted the ministry done by the locals who knew the culture, language, and tradition. It was a joy to go out and love young people in the way I knew Christ loved me. Chuck cared more about individuals than the work that they were doing."

—Mesfin Abera

"One summer, when Chuck and Linda were back in the U.S., I had the opportunity to live with Mesfin in their Kore house. One afternoon, Mesfin and I were walking down the hill to get a cab and go to work. Because she used to give food and money to the kids in the neighborhood, kids would assume that everyone in the car driving by was Linda, and they would scream their lungs out "Leenda, Leenda!"

and just follow the car. That's how famous she was in Kore. Great heart. And the other thing I will never forget about Linda is, while we were still living at the Church, we lived in a house built from thin metal sheets. It was really cold at night and really hot in the daytime. Linda knew this and came and gave us a bunch of blankets, so we could stay warm at night."

—**Hailu Tirusew**

From "Kore kids" in the first Young Life club in Addis Ababa:
"One day, while I was trying to find food by the trash dump in a place called Kore, Chuck approached and said 'Hi' to me. I did not expect the greeting from him, because he didn't look like me and that shocked me to death. My life was very, very difficult. With a very friendly manner, he told me about the Gospel and hugged me without worrying about my dirty clothes or that the food I was eating was from the trash dump. After that, Chuck used to come to my house twice a week to talk to me about Jesus."

—**Tilahun**

"He never walked without a Bible in his hands. Like a car doesn't move without tires, Chuck doesn't leave home without a Bible."

—**Yonas**

"After meeting Chuck, I was excited to tell my friends about him. A week later, Chuck came back to my neighborhood looking for me, which surprised me. I invited him to come to my home; Chuck was happy to do it and became the only American to ever visit my house. Although the Ethiopian traditional food could be very spicy, Chuck was willing to eat what was offered to him to show his respect to my family and culture."

—**Abebaw**

"When I told Chuck I was a comedian, he was very happy. He told me he loves comedy and he does skits at Young Life club. His jokes were very funny. Within ten minutes after I met him, he walked around the club greeting everyone. When you talked to him, he really listened to you and didn't just wander away. Even though he didn't speak the language, he would still listen to you and show you he cares. He's very easy to talk to, just like Linda."

—**Teddy**

"The entire time I have known him, I have never heard of him talk about money and the things of this world. He loves to give what he has."

—**Eshetu**

"I come from a very poor family. I was always tired and sick. I spent most of my life by the city's trash dump trying to find food. I had never thought about my future and didn't know what that was. I was hopeless. But the Lord used Chuck to turn that around. He loved me, told me the Gospel, and cared for me. This was the first time I had seen a white person come to the dumpster to talk to me and I was amazed. This was a place where people died. People didn't care about other people, and Chuck took a risk to come tell me this. God was good giving Linda to him. She's an amazing woman and loves everyone, too."

—**Ababi**

"Before I met Chuck and Linda, I hated my life. They immediately accepted me and showed me love. They told me about this guy named Jesus and how He loved me and died for me. They told me Jesus would get rid of my sorrow and change it into joy if I allowed Him to come into my life. I am whole because of Chuck and I thank God for him every day. To this day, I have not met anyone who exemplifies Jesus like Chuck."

—**Lidet**

From a faithful supporter of the work:

"One Christmas, as a family, we decided we'd like to financially support someone Chuck and Linda were working with, so I asked Chuck if there was someone he knew we could help. His response startled me. He said there were many people we could financially help but to really help we should come and visit. This made absolutely no sense to me. The thousands of dollars we would spend on plane tickets to come over and visit could surely feed many people, I said to myself. So, for almost a year I protested to Chuck, but he never changed his mind.

"Finally, in 2005, I decided we should take Chuck's advice and make a trip to Ethiopia... and my life will never be the same. I have made rich, rich, lifelong friendships, and I have come to know my God and Father in a way I never could have imagined. I return there every year, and it's become my second home. Chuck taught me through his example that my relationship with God and people are so much more valuable than money. Money doesn't help people as much as God helps people to love people. The greatest thing we can give others is the love of Jesus."

—Kip Vaile

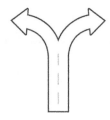

Chapter 12

A NEW VISION

"Do we have any plans for today?"

During the early 2000s, while in the midst of making great strides in the work in Ethiopia, Chuck began to notice changes in his health. From ringing in his ears to chronic fatigue to struggles with his memory, he recognized something was "off."

What's Wrong with Chuck?

For years, I had often had minor memory lapses; I could even use these to great comedic effect—how many times during club talks had I patted my chest looking for my glasses I thought were hanging around my neck, when they were in fact perched upon my head? Amidst the laughter, the audience was left wondering, "Was he truly searching for them or just pulling our leg in his self-deprecating way?"

Over time, though, the struggles with my memory seemed to increase, and those around me grew concerned. In the early 2000s, doctor visits revealed a grim diagnosis: I most likely had Alzheimer's.

The family, of course, was heartbroken upon hearing the news.

"My dad and I have always been close," Hollie said. "He's always been hilarious and inspiring at the same time—very easy to be with. I didn't have children, and it broke my heart as I always looked forward to being a mom someday, and my kids knowing their Grandpa. I felt devastated thinking I may never have a family and kids someday like I hoped, and if I did, they would never really know my dad."

Corresponding with "a Smart Kid"

The diagnosis, however, didn't keep me from living out what I sensed God was calling me to do. I still continued ministering in Ethiopia and caring for Chuckie during my son's last years.

During this time, I corresponded regularly with my lifelong friend, Bill Malarkey. We had known each other since middle school, attended Young Life together while at Mt. Lebanon, and served side by side on work crew at Frontier Ranch.

One reason for my emails to Bill, other than just two friends connecting, is that Bill is Professor Emeritus of Internal Medicine at the Ohio State University Wexner Medical Center; in other words, Bill knows his stuff, and that stuff revolves around the brain.

Bill and I also shared one other past activity: we spent countless hours playing football together in high school and at Pitt. In Bill's professional opinion, it was injuries from the many hits in those games and practices that caused my memory issues.

What follows are two emails I sent to Bill about my symptoms...

Hi Bill,

We just got word from the doctor that Chuckie has cancer (lump in throat) and he will have it cut out in the next few weeks. This will keep us here for a while and we are happy to be with him.

About my Alzheimer's. My head rings continually. I don't know if that has to do with Alzheimer's or not. This has been for a couple of years. I am tired a lot and feel like laying down. My motivation is low. It is hard to have goals which I am used to living by. Is this what Alzheimer's does? What should I do to fight it? I thank the Lord and do not fight that I have it. I have had so much, and this is not something I feel badly about. I want to deal with it in the right way. I just don't know how to live with it and what to accept or not accept. You're a smart kid. What is your advice?

Love,

Chuck (6/3/2005)

Hi Bill,

You are great. Thanks for your note. I am not concerned about Alzheimer's. I have lived life more than I deserve and seem to have had all the breaks. I am receiving this as a gift of the Lord. It is my turn to trust Him and be faithful.

Chuckie is terrified but seems to be accepting it. He will have an operation soon to have the cancer removed from his salivary gland and part of his jawbone. They will use a transplant from bone in his leg for his jaw. He will be in surgery for 12 hours. The radiation following will be for seven weeks.

Thank God for doctors and new procedures.

You are a treasured friend,

Chuck (6/6/2005)

Studies have shown that once diagnosed with Alzheimer's, patients typically live an average of **eight to ten more years**. This meant I *might* live to see the year 2014. Yet even so, what would be the quality of life, with the debilitating effects of the disease?

A Different Diagnosis

It is now March 2018 and Chuck is very much with us! At seventy-nine, he continues to struggle with short-term memory loss, but he's quite lucid when it comes to recalling many events from childhood and beyond.

"No one thinks my dad has Alzheimer's anymore," Hollie said. "It is impossible to know for sure until he dies, but we all suspect his condition is from football. A direct quote from my dad is, 'My memory is not good these days (football concussions... wouldn't trade it).'

"We all kept waiting for my dad to get worse and not know us and not be himself, but to our great surprise and joy, thirteen years later he is for the most part still himself and knows and loves all of us... including his seven grandchildren who have only known him during his struggle with his memory.

Chuck's neurologist confirmed he has a form of dementia, but it doesn't present itself as Alzheimer's because he has not progressed like a typical Alzheimer's patient. He has been on memory medication for several years.

"He doesn't care that he has zero short-term memory," Hollie explained. "He's perfectly content. He learned to be content in all circumstances when he was in Ethiopia after college with Don and Lyda McClure. Don had shared 1 Thessalonians 5:18 ('Give thanks in all circumstances; for this is God's will for you in Christ Jesus') many times and ever since, my dad has strived to live this out. It's become one of THE verses of his life. Our dad lives his life moment by moment knowing wholeheartedly that more important than his health is his relationship with Christ."

Chuck's "Secret" Weapon

How has Chuck managed to stay as sharp as he has, when so many others seem to go into a quick decline? The answer may surprise you.

"Part of the process of his dementia is ongoing inflammation," said Bill, who has spent years studying how football injuries to the brain can cause memory loss. "My research and that of others have shown that positive inputs into our lives like Scripture reading and prayer have anti-inflammatory properties. In contrast, worry, fear and anxiety accelerate inflammation."

In other words, Hollie said, "Bill believes *what's protected our dad's brain from getting worse over these past fourteen years or so is his relationship with Jesus and his discipline of reading Scripture every day.*"

In January 2017, Chuck visited his neurologist, who had been treating him since his initial diagnosis. Linda shared with her Bill's belief that Chuck's memory and spirit hasn't declined as rapidly as most patients with similar issues because for sixty years he's been waking up early and spending time in prayer, reading the Word, and memorizing Scripture.

"After the neurologist listened to our mom share," Hollie smiled, "she said she's going to start spending time in the Scriptures herself!"

"I'm not just saying this," the neurologist continued. "Chuck really has encouraged me to start spending time in Scripture, so I'll be more positive and content and happy when I'm older. I want to have Chuck's attitude as I age. I'm amazed at his joy and contentment and how funny he is with me!"

"She also explained our dad is highly unusual because typically there is anger and depression when you have dementia and memory issues," Hollie said, "and almost always you have to go on anxiety and antidepressant medicine, but he hasn't. She sees the value of Mom and Dad having each other as a couple and believes this is a big plus for both of them."

Perfect Companions

Cliché as it may sound, Linda and Chuck have only grown in their love and need for one another. Back in 2012, Linda became very sick. "We thought she had a stroke," Hollie said, "and after some time she was diagnosed with myasthenia gravis (a chronic autoimmune neuromuscular disease)."

Realizing the difficulties in trying to live on their own, Linda and Chuck soon sold their house. The two now spend time between Josh's home in Virginia and Hollie's in Tennessee.

Hollie said, "My dad is in great physical condition with zero short-term memory; while Mom's mentally sharp but can only walk very short distances before needing to sit down. They take care of each other in a beautiful way. My mom has to manage everything from a practical standpoint and my dad brings her whatever she needs and helps with all of the physical labor. He can't remember she's sick, but he's still so loving.

"It's lonely for Mom. She doesn't have someone to talk to about her day because he doesn't remember it. No longer can she share life with my dad in a way that they can make new memories, have shared experiences, and reminisce together. It's isolating, too, because they both love people and being part of a community and having fellowship. Despite all of this, my mom trucks on with her faith and huge heart.

The companionship goes deeper than just conversations. Hollie said, "They share an amazing history of life together and that alone gives them strength. Also, sharing their hope in Christ and praying for their family draws them close! My mom doesn't want fear of the future or sadness in the present to be the center of her life. She loves my dad more than ever and once again reminds us of her call to love and care for my dad!"

Every day is an opportunity for Hollie to choose to view things from a positive perspective. She knows full well that if Chuck and Linda were healthy and able to live on their own, both Josh's family and her own would not have enjoyed so many wonderful memories, experiences, and time spent together with them.

What follows are some of these memories about their dad and grandpa...

This Is Who My Dad Is!

"My dad is consistent if nothing else," Josh said. "He's always been a man of prayer. Yodit and I have three beautiful children, Serena (eleven), Aman (nine), and Leah (seven). When we were expecting Leah, we learned she had Dandy-Walker syndrome and was missing chromosome material and would most likely be severely handicapped in many ways. She was able to come home with us from the hospital right away, and we were thrilled. Later that year, however, things went terribly wrong. One of the darkest times in my life was when Leah was at Children's Hospital having surgery to install a shunt in her head to drain the excess fluid building up. Doctors told us she was close to death.

"It's a terrible feeling to see your eight-month-old daughter connected to all this equipment and tubes going every which way. I'd been going into the bathroom to get on my knees and beg for my daughter's life. When Leah's health took a turn for the worse and things didn't look good, I called Dad. When he got on the phone, words wouldn't come out of my mouth. I was too emotional and couldn't tell him how dark things felt and just how dire the situation was. He could tell I was struggling, and after a few moments of my incoherent emotional sounds, he began to pray for me and for Leah. That was his default and it was beautiful; it was just what I needed at that moment and it encouraged me immensely. This is who he is."

A Special Grandpa

"I'm going on thirteen years of marriage and we have four children— triplets plus an adorable baby brother," Hollie said. "The gift today is

*Chuck and Linda's grandchildren celebrating their
Grandma's seventieth birthday and Chuck and Linda's
fiftieth wedding anniversary, in the summer of 2017.*

that my dad lives 100 percent in the moment. My dad is all there with
our kids giving them his undivided attention for long periods of times.
He plays with them and reads the Bible to them, asking them questions,
and adding his commentary on Jesus… and he wonders why he's so tired
at night!"

Hollie acknowledges that her initial broken heart at imagining
her children not getting to experience the real Chuck was unnecessary.
"As Jesus says in Matthew 6:21, 'For where your treasure is, there your
heart will be also.' As you can see, they know my dad because his 'heart
memory' is there 100 percent…"

"Grandpa taught me God has a sense of humor, because Jesus told
stories to help people know God's Word. Grandpa taught me that back
in Jesus' time the houses weren't built very well, and friends could break
roofs to lower their friends to Jesus. That is how important God's Word
is and Jesus… people would break roofs to get to Jesus and to get their
friends to Jesus. I love that Grandpa is funny and has a child's heart."

—**Jake Birckhead**, ten years old

"Grandpa taught me the story of Bartimaeus and that everything is possible with God—that Jesus can do stuff for me and other people. Jesus healed Bartimaeus and he was blind. I love that my Grandpa knows a lot about Jesus and God and that he plays football in his sleep."

—**Charlie Birckhead**, ten years old

"I love that Grandpa loves dogs and nature like I do. He has a great love for God. He reads the Bible in the morning and throughout the day. I love football like Grandpa and love that he was a great football player. He is really fun and funny!"

—**Kaylee Birckhead**, ten years old

"Grandpa is funny and nice and friendly. He is funny by making me laugh with jokes and he does Itsy Bitsy Spider up to my armpit and then tickles me. He has taught me Jesus loves me more than I love me."

—**Sam Birckhead**, eight years old

And, of course, Josh's kids are just as crazy about their Grandpa:

"I love that my Grandpa is always so happy to see me. He is funny and fun to be with. He taught me to be able to recite "Prinderella" and helps me memorize Bible verses."

—**Serena Reinhold**, eleven years old

"I love that Grandpa plays with me and makes me laugh. My favorite joke of his is 'Do you serve crabs? Yes, we serve everybody.' I also like that he loves Jesus."

—**Aman Reinhold**, nine years old

PURE CHUCK (circa 1970s)

"During Chuck's sabbatical, Doug Holladay, Chuck, and I spent one memorable night in a very old hotel in Ethiopia. They only had one room with one bed, which we three had to share. This alone promised an interesting night! We put Chuck in the middle, Doug and I on either side. It was hot, so we left the window open, not knowing that below the window was the trash area.

We began reflecting on our day, with many comical comments by both guys. I was at their mercy and couldn't stop laughing. The lights were out, and we wanted to try to sleep, until this buzzy sound started bombarding each of us. MOSQUITOES! Millions of them, buzzing and dive bombing us. We took turns holding the flashlight and swatting these monsters. Doug and Chuck began assigning names to each mosquito; it was miserable, but they made it too funny. It went on forever. Finally, morning came and the wall next to the bed was covered with splotches of blood and dead mosquitoes! Gross... needless to say we were exhausted but knew we couldn't stay another night there. I will never forget that night I shared a bed with both Chuck and Doug!"

—Linda

Influencing the Influencers!

While Chuck's world may be a little more confined these days, his wisdom continues to impact future generations of believers. Chuck has been around the block long enough to have known every president of Young Life, from founder Jim Rayburn, who was the president until 1964 through Newt Crenshaw, who became Young Life's sixth president in 2016.

In March 2017, Newt made it a point to have lunch with Chuck. The meeting was significant to Newt, who shared some of Chuck's wisdom with the entire mission…

"We all need to stay close to our Lord and pray that He would speak through us in every encounter we have. So many of you have been praying for me to 'abide in Christ' as I have shared that prayer request in many places over the past year. I pray the same for each of you! It is clear from the Scriptures that trials and persecution should 'push us up against the Lord,' as Chuck Reinhold put it to Wiley Scott [Young Life's Senior Vice President of the Eastern Division] and me when we visited with him in Washington D.C." (From the July 24, 2017 edition of Young Life's *Monday Morning* newsletter)

Newt, in spending a great deal of time learning about the history of the mission he's now entrusted with leading, has become a big fan of the many people, like Chuck, who've left their large imprint upon Young Life. He's in good company.

The Adventure Continues

Usually Chuck's first question every morning is, "Do we have any plans for today?"

"He's always ready for adventure, time with people, or just a trip to Walmart," Linda said. "I tell him 'no plans' or 'maybe we'll pick up our grandkids from school.' No matter, he just wanted to know. This routine question will continue through the morning.

"What makes me know Chuck is still himself is his use of humor. His timing is amazing, and he applies it perfectly. He just won't remember what he said and why we're laughing."

Chuck and Linda have known each other for fifty-five years and been married for all but five of those. Linda wouldn't trade a moment of it. "I knew very early on God called me to love and marry Chuck. Many would question why I didn't have my own ambition and plans. I have never wavered in my purpose and dedication to be Chuck's wife and helper. That's not to say it's always been easy; we've had our struggles, but never enough to give up. What a privilege and joy I've had to be his wife, full of many highs and lows but always led by his faith and vision.

"Loving him has been a great adventure and taken me all over the world! I believe with my whole heart that God prepared me for this special time in our lives."

With his Bible and trusty tools like the *Topical Memory System* and *Search the Scriptures* by his side, Chuck continues to greet each day with his special time with the Lord, Linda said. "This routine of his continues to give me confidence and comfort in my own life. Most of his thoughts refer back to childhood and his time with Don McClure in Ethiopia. He reads a lot and loves sitting in his recliner listening to hymns!"

Chuck and Linda with all of their grandchildren (except their precious youngest granddaughter, Leah) at Young Life Rockbridge Alum Springs 25th Anniversary celebration in May 2018!

Chuck's journey from a man of great leadership and vision to one with very limited outreach could cause tremendous sadness, Linda said, but Chuck never exhibits disappointment or frustration—only thankfulness. "He realizes he struggles with his memory, but this is just an inconvenience for him, not a hardship. It's embarrassing how many times a day he tells me he loves me! He loves his kids and grandkids, the greatest part of who we are. And despite his memory issues, Chuck still remembers Corrie and Chuckie!

"Chuck's life might be lived in a smaller environment, but his heart and mind continue to be full of meaning, joy and life. He simply says, 'In Christ we all have a life worth living!'"

Principles Learned Along the Way:

Make Scripture memory a lifetime habit. *How can a young person stay on the path of purity? By living according to your Word. I have hidden your Word in my heart that I might not sin against you.* (Ps. 119:9, 11)

"Chuck and I were walking to lunch and we were going over Topical Memory System verses. Chuck had this faux leather card holder with his cards in it. I said, 'Oh Chuck, that holder is so cool!' Without hesitation, he took the cards out and said, 'Here, I want you to have it!' I still have my verses in that card holder to this day with the cards from training thirty-plus years ago."

—Rick Rogan

Wake up early to be with the Father. *Very early in the morning, while it was still dark, Jesus got up, left the house and went off to a solitary place, where he praye*d. (Mark 1:35)

"The last few years I've taken college students to the men's weekend at Rockbridge. The highlight for guys has been Saturday morning when

75–100 of us cram into the parlor just to hear Chuck talk about life. Chuck would say something like, '…did you guys know Jesus got up early to be with the Father? In Mark 1:35, Jesus got up very early… Why wouldn't we want to do that? It's been the most important thing I've done in my life. If Jesus needed to start his day that way, I probably should too!'

"A few minutes would pass, and Chuck would be telling a different story and interrupt himself again with the same thought about waking up early to be with Jesus (almost verbatim). The second and third time it happened, I, along with everyone else, would shake my head politely, pretending to hear it for the first time. The fourth and fifth time he did it, a smile crossed my face, and I really sensed God was speaking to the room through Chuck. No one could have sat in that room and not left with a deep sense of the importance of meeting daily with our Creator. Chuck lived out that discipline faithfully and is still passionate about it to this day."

—**Dave Sloop**, Young Life staff

"When I was in middle school, I tried out for the high school freshmen football team. This was scary for me and I had tremendous anxiety, which would be a recurring theme in my life. My dad told me to concentrate on the fundamentals of blocking and tackling. Listen to the coaches and focus on doing the basic things as best as I could. That is exactly what I did and ended up making the team and being the only eighth grader to start for the ninth-grade team. I know it is a small thing, and I only bring it up because it speaks to a larger force in my dad's life.

"He always focused on the fundamentals of prayer and spending time with the Lord. He'd wake up long before the sun would come up and spend a couple of hours praying and reading the Word of God. I remember being a little kid, probably five or six years old, and waking up early seeing the light shine from under the door of our den. Sometimes I would open the door and see him reading his Bible. He would always give me a big smile, shake his shoulders, and move his arms with excitement that I was there. Focus on the fundamentals and the rest will follow.

"When I first arrived at Philadelphia Bible College, I had a real problem with anxiety again. I can remember the example Dad used when I was having a hard time getting to know people and wanting to come home. He told me the story of the priests who were carrying the Ark of the Covenant into the Jordan River and how it wasn't until the priest stepped into the water that the waters down river were held back. The priest had to take the first step and trust the Lord."

—**Josh Reinhold**

Chuck and Linda wanted to close with just one more taste of Chuck's passion for God's Word. What follows is a letter Chuck often sent out around New Year's…

The Thirty-Day Challenge

I am passing on to you a gift given to me years ago that has contributed greatly and wonderfully to my life. Many of you have received this gift before, and I am offering it to you again this year. This gift comes free and like many gifts, it is useless unless you use it. This gift is also very expensive and actually cost Jesus Christ His life, which was His pleasure. He died on the cross for our sins in order to bring us to God (John 3:16, John 1:12, 1 John 5:11–12).

This gift comes in the way of a challenge in order to help us truly receive the gift of daily relationship with Him. The gift comes free, but it must be received and with its responsibilities.

The gift is this, a close and meaningful daily walk with the Lord. This enjoyment of the gift is grounded in the "THIRTY-DAY CHALLENGE."

The "Challenge" is this: that we commit ourselves to meet with our Lord Jesus Christ every morning for thirty straight days by reading a portion of Scripture and asking the Lord to give us something to apply to our lives that day. If we miss a day, then we start over until we meet with Him for thirty straight days. If we do this, chances are we'll never quit, and our lives will continue to grow in our Lord Jesus Christ. During this special time, look for an answer to this question. "What does He want me to be, feel, or do today?" Then write out in a sentence what He wants for us to be that day, as specifically as we can. Then, as we pray for the day and our cares, ask God to help us apply the truth that we learned that morning from His Word.

That is a pretty exciting challenge, isn't it? The payoff is all that we truly desire. It presses us to listen to Him, to obey Him, and to enjoy His fellowship. John 15:5 is one of many places in Scripture that He promises abundance in our relationship with Him: "I am the vine; you are the branches. If you remain in me and I in you, you will bear much fruit; apart from me you can do nothing."

Many of you are on your 500th straight day or more. My gift to you is the "thirty-day challenge." To start today and carefully enjoy thirty straight days with the Lord with renewed vigor, sensitivity, and desire to obey. Then keep on going with renewed understanding. You will be blessed to bless others.

You might want to take a paragraph or two of Psalm 119 each day until you finish the Psalm.

Each time this Psalm mentions something about the Word of God, write it down. It will enrich you and give you abundant reasons to continue your thirty-day challenge for the rest of your life.

Your friend in Jesus Christ,

Chuck Reinhold

AFTERWORD

By Dr. Lee Corder

In the spring of 1973, while in my first job with the U.S. government, I attended something called Young Life leadership at the invitation of a new friend, Young Life staff person Tuck Knupp. Although I had no clue then, that little meeting changed forever the trajectory of my life.

Leading the time was a man named Chuck Reinhold, and this first meeting started a relationship with a guy who's impacted my life more than anyone except my wife and parents. (Though a pastor's son who was committed to not being a professional minister, I found a real calling and partner, my wife Paula, with whom I've walked this remarkable journey of faith for over forty-five years.)

I laugh as I now remember how enthusiastically Chuck responded to a couple of my answers during Bible study. As an expressive, I'm never afraid to speak, but I cringe when I consider the shallow kinds of insights I probably offered that day. It is pretty clear in hindsight my answers did not merit the encouraging responses Chuck offered. But man, did he draw me in! I was hooked, and my life has truly never been the same.

A few years later our paths intersected in a much more significant relationship as I had come on Young Life staff and didn't have anyone to train me. Although Chuck was serving full time at the National Presbyterian Church, he still graciously took me under his wing; we spent several hours together every Friday morning in our own one-on-one training experience. I'll never forget those meetings at his office. We'd study a passage of Scripture, review our memory verses, and talk at length about our own journey with Jesus. (It's hard to fake your memory verses if you're the only student in the class.) Having those few hours together always gave us enough time to talk about some core issue of leadership or ministry. But those conversations always flowed out of the backdrop of Scripture application.

Fast forward several years, when Chuck became my direct supervisor, serving first as regional director and later as my divisional director in Young Life's Eastern Division. I don't have the space to recall all the gifts of training and wisdom Chuck imparted. Suffice it to say that, if there are any positive expressions in my own leadership today, they owe a huge amount to his profound influence. Disciplines of goalsetting, experiential learning and group leadership, the power of purpose statements and unifying principles, the importance of first things first, all flow from Chuck's leadership model.

He lived out lessons about respect for other ministries and the larger kingdom of God as we joined in Campus Crusade evangelism training and used the Navigators' *Topical Memory System* and *Design for Discipleship* books as crucial tools in our education in discipleship.

Later, I was privileged to see Chuck's vision and development of the new start-up in Ethiopia. I'll never forget Ethiopian training days where love, affirmation, reflection, confession, forgiveness, Scripture, and sharing shaped the first generation of a movement that's exploded in that nation. Chuck's mentorship of Steve Larmey, the current senior vice president of Africa/Middle East, helped lay the foundation of that work which today impacts twenty-two nations across that remarkable continent.

In these last years with Chuck's issues with short-term memory, we've found new ways to use his remarkable gifts with a whole new generation. One can't help but observe the sweet spirit of Chuck's genuine love for Jesus and the passionate way he talks about the privilege we have of meeting every day with the Lord. It's been a remarkable gift to watch young twenty-somethings sit in the room and be struck again by his call to each one to take time to experience intimacy with Jesus Himself. What fun to hear millennial leaders describe how they're impacted by Chuck's love for the Scriptures and time in the Savior's presence.

After all these years, he continues to impact young people because of his own faithful journey with the One who called him every day to trust Him with all his heart, mind, strength, and soul. For Chuck, this walking with Jesus is "real living."

—**Dr. Lee Corder**, Senior Vice President, Young Life International

Appendix
CHUCK'S CORE PRINCIPLES

Jesus replied: "Love the Lord your God with all your heart and with all your soul and with all your mind. This is the first and greatest commandment. And the second is like it: Love your neighbor as yourself. All the Law and Prophets hang on these two commandments." (Matt. 22:37–40)

1. **There is nothing more important to me than my relationship with Christ.** (John 15:5; Phil. 3:8; Phil. 1:21; Matt. 6:33; Luke 9:23; Luke 14:33)
2. **Obedience and living outside your comfort zone is the "key" to experiencing Christ.** (John 14:21; Heb. 11:6)
3. **I become what I think about. What am I thinking about?** (Rom. 12:2; Jer. 2:5)

4. **I communicate in over 750 ways other than verbal. What am I saying?** (1 John 3:18; 2 Cor. 2:14–16, 3:1–3; John 13:34–35; 1 Thess. 4:11–12)

5. **I live for Christ when no one is around.** (Col. 3:23–24; 2 Chron. 16:9)

6. **Nothing eternal is accomplished except through prayer.** (Matt. 6:6; John 15:7; 2 Chron. 7:14; Jer. 33:3)

7. **Meditating on God's Word and listening with obedience is the "key" to success.** (Josh. 1:8; Deut. 17:18–20; Ps. 119)

8. **Humility and serving others is the "key" to greatness.** (Mark 10:35–45; Mark 9:33–35; Phil. 2:1–11)

9. **Consistent, meaningful fellowship is a non-negotiable for growth in Christ.** (Heb. 10:24–25; Matt. 18:20; Acts 2:42–47; Prov. 27:17; Ps. 122:1)

10. **Am I doing things that I would never do without Christ—or do I rely on myself?** (Phil. 4:13; Heb. 11:6; Exod; 3; 2 Cor. 1:8–9; 5:15)

EVEN MORE (!) PRINCIPLES LEARNED ALONG THE WAY...

- **Live a life of continual confession and forgiveness.**

One verse that became a favorite the first time I heard it was 1 John 1:9, which says, "If we confess our sins, He is faithful and just and will forgive us our sins and purify us from all unrighteousness." I have been thankful for that verse ever since and have used it two or three times (times a million). He has never disappointed me.

- **Keep short accounts with God (and others).**

I come more quickly to ask for love and forgiveness from our Savior and others, to set things right and then do all I can to live to the praise of His glory.

- **The Lord plus nothing is everything. (Phil. 3)**
- **See your life with an Acts 1:8 worldview.**

Do you believe this verse? What is *your* personal Jerusalem, Judea, and Samaria?

- **Always be talking with others about how they're doing *with the Lord*.**

Their journey of faith is more important than their work.

- **Invite people to come and see. (John 1:39)**
- **Humor builds relationships.**

In humor, the Gospel is expressed in unique and powerful ways:

- o **Love:** Making others laugh is a ministry of love that prepares the way for the Gospel.
- o **Forgiveness:** As we laugh, we release the tension that comes with unrealized holiness.
- o **Relationship:** The people we laugh with are the ones we appreciate most.
- o **Freedom:** G. K. Chesterton said, "Angels can fly because they can take themselves lightly."
- o **Healing:** Humor and laughter are God's healing gifts to us. Just ask Abraham and Sarah or their son Isaac (meaning, "he will laugh").
- o **Trust:** Good humor undergirds our willingness to trust Jesus for transforming impact rather than our own cleverness.
- **What we are told has low impact. What we discover for ourselves has high impact.**
- **Discipling a few leads to reaching the many:**
  1. Jesus's primary investment of time and teaching during His three-year public ministry was into his disciples. He built His ministry through them and He is our model today for how to build ministry and how to build people.
  2. A group of teenagers (Campaigners!) who love Christ with passion, love one another in Christ, are taught the power of prayer for the lost and who deeply care that their non-believing friends know Him, is the best formula to start and grow an effective club. We start club when THEY are

ready to come, invite and bring friends—when they are passionate about a club in their school.

3. These Campaigner kids (who will have their ups and downs just like the disciples) essentially become our "junior leaders," our partners in ministry. They're positioned to reach far more kids (under the guidance of the actual staff and volunteer leaders in the club) than we could ever reach without them—they OWN the club with us. It may take some extra time at the front end to establish their buy-in, but as our friends in Africa have taught us, "The slow way really is the fast way."

4. The best leadership development tool for lifelong ministry is for them to own the Young Life ministry in their school under our Christ-like, nurturing, and strategic leadership. It is the best strategy for starting a new club and the best strategy to develop new, eager Young Life leaders once they graduate from high school.

From Tuck Knupp:

- Heb. 11:6, *For without faith it is impossible to please God...*

"Chuck is the very embodiment of that verse. For him 'really living' is living by faith. It was faith that drove him to Rochester to plant Young Life."

- If you act enthusiastic you will be enthusiastic!
- Motivate people to be their best by painting a picture of who they were that's just a little beyond the reality of their actual performance. Then affirm them for it as if it was true of them.

"The effect—If Chuck believed that about me then I would knock myself out trying to live up to his opinion."

- The formula for training successful leaders was always: *Fellowship, Doctrine, and Vision.* Get leaders together and create a caring fellowship among them, teach them how to love and follow Christ, and then cast vision for reaching high school kids.

"The two key verses on this for Chuck were:"

1. *I looked for someone among them who would build up the wall and stand before me in the gap on behalf of the land so I would not have to destroy it, but I found no one.* (Ezek. 22:30)

"Chuck would call this the 'saddest verse in the Bible' and then challenge us to be that one the Lord could count on."

2. *For the eyes of the Lord range throughout the earth to strengthen those whose hearts are fully committed to him.* (2 Chron. 16:9)

"Again, God is constantly looking for that man or woman ready to be totally committed to his purposes—will you be that one?"

From Doug Holladay:

- The more you give things away, the more they come back to you.

"Following one lacrosse practice my junior year, I asked Chuck whether I could be the president if I were a follower of Jesus. Now, many leaders are not comfortable when their protégés spend time with others, but that day, he arranged for me to meet Doug Coe, another important mentor who exposed me to an even larger world."

- All are broken and insecure and need reassurance.

"When Chuck starts a meeting, he has those in attendance turn to one another and quietly utter, 'You're forgiven.' Wow. Who thinks like that? Jesus and his dogged follower Chuck Reinhold certainly did."

BIBLE STUDIES
Jesus and His Worship Time
Mark 1:35–38

Very early in the morning, while it was still dark, Jesus got up, left the house and went off to a solitary place, where he prayed. Simon and his companions went to look for him, and when they found him, they exclaimed: "Everyone is looking for you!"

Jesus replied, "Let us go somewhere else—to the nearby villages—so I can preach there also. That is why I have come." (Mark 1:35–38)

What do you think the point of the passage is?

Options:
We need to get up and start the day with the Lord before we do anything. That is what Jesus did and anything good enough for Him is good enough for us.

He had made an impact and the people were there waiting for him. I think it's this:

If He hadn't met with His Father, He might have done the wrong thing!

He might have stayed and met the needs of those around Him… and never got to the business of going to the cross for us. The Father reminded Him that He was there to get to the towns that were not yet touched. (Get on your way to Jerusalem and the cross.) If He hadn't met with His Father. He might have the whole world but be submitted to Satan. (Matt. 4:8)

But look how tempting it must have been. "Everyone is looking for you…"

("Okay, let's go to work. Let's heal those people.")

Blind men, lepers, paralyzed people. Could anything be more lovingly important? Would anyone call Him a lousy Christian if He healed the people?

("Jesus, there you are spending time with God and you could have healed twenty-five people in the same amount of time.")

How about when Jesus was on the cross and says, "It is finished!" If I was a blind man I would have said, "What about me? You *aren't* finished!"

Are you busier than Jesus? You only need to do what God has called you to do. Do you know what it is? Ask Him.

Some of you are too busy for God and too busy to do what God wants you to do. *And people are praising you for it.*

You are going down this street for contact work and God wants you to go down the other. You are making this phone call and God wants you to make the other.

Conclusion:

Let's build our house of worship, our time with God, listening to Him, confessing, and receiving forgiveness, acknowledging He is God and we are not. Let Him free up our schedule to do what He wants. Building our self-esteem by being what He wants us to be and not what others want us to be.

"The So What":

1. There is nothing more important to our ministry than our relationship with Jesus Christ.
2. We communicate in 750 ways other than verbal.
3. In 2 Cor. 2:15, Paul says we are the perfume of Christ in a letter written by Christ.
4. In the Sermon on the Mount, Jesus talks about praying, giving, fasting... These things are all hidden. No one sees you doing them. *This* is where the reward is.

BIBLE STUDIES
The Centurion's Servant
Luke 7:1–10

When Jesus had finished saying all this to the people who were listening, he entered Capernaum. There a centurion's servant, whom his master valued highly, was sick and about to die. The centurion heard of Jesus and sent some elders of the Jews to him, asking him to come and heal his servant. When they came to Jesus, they pleaded earnestly with him, "This man deserves to have you do this, because he loves our nation and has built our synagogue." So Jesus went with them.

He was not far from the house when the centurion sent friends to say to him: 'Lord, don't trouble yourself, for I do not deserve to have you come under my roof. That is why I did not even consider myself worthy to come to you. But say the word, and my servant will be healed. For I myself am a man under authority, with soldiers under me. I tell this one, "Go," and he goes; and that one, "Come," and he comes. I say to my servant, "Do this," and he does it.'

When Jesus heard this, he was amazed at him, and turning to the crowd following him, he said, "I tell you, I have not found such great faith even in Israel." Then the men who had been sent returned to the house and found the servant well. (Luke 7:1–10)

What a passage to tell us what God is like as we see Him in His Son Jesus Christ. He had authority to do all things. By His thoughts He can heal a person He does not see or even know his location or condition. He was all-powerful. Yet at the same time, He was a humble servant submitting Himself to a pagan Gentile soldier and some proud Jews!

One group came to Jesus telling Him the centurion deserved to have Jesus heal his servant. The centurion sent word he was not deserving of even having Jesus in his house. He never doubted, though, that Jesus could heal his servant

Here is how not to ask God to do something: "We deserve to have you do it because we built a church and we love Christians." This flies in the truth of who we really are, helpless and hopeless sinners deserving only the wrath of God. (Rom. 3:23, 6:23) But Jesus is so eager to respond to faith even when it appears to be so little or with so little understanding. He must have felt the centurion knew something about Him to ask the question of healing his servant so clearly. I think Jesus saw the man's faith in His (divine) ability and the man's love for his servant. Maybe, also, he saw the centurion's humility in not coming himself. Also, he might have seen this opportunity to draw Jews to the truth of who He was.

Also, what does it say about a Roman centurion that he would be drawn to the Jews in love and build them a synagogue. Jesus must have seen the centurion as a man who was seeking the truth of God. My guess is that Roman soldiers, especially centurions, were not natural friends with the Jews. In fact, since they were the occupiers, they were distrusted and disliked. (Like the Jewish soldiers occupying Gaza.)

I wonder if he was not a wonderful curiosity for Jesus—the soldier in authority whose heart went against the grain of society. He loved the Jews. He demonstrated it with time and money in building the synagogue, which demonstrated his desire for God. And he loved a servant. That had to have touched Christ's heart. The "deserved" part did not sway Jesus to come. In fact, it was the centurion's actions of humility in not coming personally that also drew Jesus. Humility draws God to us.

Also, another reason Jesus was drawn to the centurion is because he just plain loved people. A slave, the enemy, the Jews. He put his money where his mouth was.

"Dear friends, let us love one another, for love comes from God. Everyone who loves has been born of God and knows God. Whoever does not love does not know God, because God is love." (1 John 4:7–8)

The centurion must have picked up the "superiority" of the Jews over Gentiles. Somehow, he must have learned that God was for the Jews first and that everyone else was inferior and undeserving of God, but that God loved all people. It was kind of like "God loves you, but He loves us better because we deserve His love." In a sense, the centurion had a better idea of the truth of God than the Jews because of the superior claim the Jews had of God and the inferior undeserving attitude the Jews gave the Gentiles in response to God. They were accurate in the way they conveyed God to the Gentiles and totally off in the way they conveyed God to themselves.

"This man deserves to have you do this, because he loves our nation and has built our synagogue." It seems they did not really care about the servant as any reason to heal him. They appealed to the centurion and his merits. It tells you what they felt about servants. Why didn't they just say, "Come, there is a servant sick and about to die"?

Unlike the leper in Matt. 8:1–5, the centurion did not wonder if Jesus loved his servant enough to heal him. He also did not consider his "unworthy" status before Jesus a barrier to Jesus' compassion of healing his servant. I think this was part of Jesus' amazement. He did not wonder "if Jesus wanted to."

Why was Jesus amazed? Why was it such great faith? In spite of knowing his unworthiness, he seemed to know that Jesus was more than willing and loving to heal a servant or anyone. He believed Jesus had the authority to do whatever He asked or commanded.

In verse 9, Jesus did not deny that He had the power to heal by His Word. He merely praised the centurion for his faith that recognized His power and authority.

Consider this thought: we are no different than the centurion. He only knew Jesus by reputation, like us. He never saw Him. It was by "prayer and faith."

Questions:

1. How would you describe the centurion? Let's be detectives. Tell me everything you know about the centurion from the passage. Remember, the Romans were the occupying force for the Jews in Israel. They were the enemy (i.e. Jewish soldiers in Gaza).

2. How would you contrast the attitude of the Jews and the attitude of the centurion in meriting Jesus' help?

3. What do you think the centurion knew about Jesus in this incident?

4. What was it about the centurion's faith that so impressed and amazed Jesus?

5. How would you describe this kind of faith for yourself?

RECOMMENDED
BOOKS AND WEBSITES

(A non-exhaustive list!)

All his life Chuck has loved books and passing them on to others to encourage their spiritual growth. "Every time he gave out a book," Jan Pascoe recalled, "it was a measured calculation of the worth it would be to the recipient if they would read it and learn from it. He gave away every book he ever had (!) with one exception—he still has his cherished *Search the Scriptures* edition from the '60s; it's pretty dog-eared, but he says it's still the most powerful book outside the Bible he's ever read."

What follows is a mere snapshot of the library Chuck used to disciple and train generations of leaders:

Basic Christianity by John Stott
Borden of Yale by Geraldine Taylor

Celebration of Discipline by Richard J. Foster

C. T. Studd: Cricketer and Pioneer by Norman Grubb

Design for Discipleship Series by The Navigators

A Diary of Private Prayer by John Baillie

Focused Lives by J. Robert Clinton

Hand Me Another Brick by Chuck Swindoll

How to Win Friends and Influence People by Dale Carnegie

Hudson Taylor's Spiritual Secret by Dr. and Mrs. Howard Taylor

Imitation of Christ by Thomas á Kempis

More than Equals: Racial Healing for the Sake of the Gospel by
    Spencer Perkins and Chris Rice

My Utmost for His Highest by Oswald Chambers

Pensées by Blaise Pascal

Power Through Prayer by E.M. Bounds

Practicing His Presence by Brother Lawrence, Frank C. Laubach

Prayer: Conversing with God by Rosalind Rinker

Psycho Cybernetics by Maxwell Maltz

Search the Scriptures by Alan M. Stibbs

Seven Habits of Highly Effective People by Stephen R. Covey

Spiritual Leadership by Oswald Sanders

Strength to Love by Martin Luther King, Jr.

The Lost Art of Disciple Making by LeRoy Eims

The Making of a Leader by Dr. J. Robert Clinton

The Master Plan of Evangelism by Robert E. Coleman

The Pursuit of God by A.W. Tozer

The Screwtape Letters by C.S. Lewis

The Spirit of the Disciplines by Dallas Willard

The Way of the Heart by Henri J. M. Nouwen

Think and Grow Rich by Napoleon Hill

Thou Givest... They Gather by Amy Carmichael

Through Gates of Splendor by Elisabeth Elliot

Time Power by Charles Hobbs

Topical Memory System by The Navigators

We Would See Jesus by Roy and Revel Hession

Books on Young Life:

Back to the Basics of Young Life by John Miller (1991)

From Bondage to Liberty: Dance Children Dance by Jim Rayburn III (2000)

It's a Sin to Bore a Kid by Char Meredith (1978)

Letters to a Young Life Leader by Bob Mitchell (2012)

Made for This: The Young Life Story by Jeff Chesemore (2015)

The Diaries of Jim Rayburn by Kit Sublett, Editor (2008)

Young Life by Emile Cailliet (1963)

Recommended Websites:

www.chuckreinhold.com

www.alifeworthlivingbook.com

ACKNOWLEDGEMENTS

On behalf of our dad, mom, and our family, we would like to express our deep gratitude to the team of people who have come alongside our dad to write this book. Our dad has had short-term memory struggles for years but continues to have 110 percent "heart memory." The ways the Lord has worked in his life are as real to him today as they were many years ago when they happened.

Our dad constantly talked about how he would love to write a book to give glory to God for his life, which he is deeply grateful for. But he knew deep down he would never be able to do this on his own because of his memory struggles. However, a few years ago God put on our hearts to help him write his book.

We would like to thank Karen Anderson, an old Young Life friend and Associate Publisher for Morgan James Publishing, and the Morgan James Publishing staff for making this book a reality. Thank you, Karen, for your friendship, encouragement, support, and for going above and beyond your job description to walk our family and the team of people helping to put this book together through the entire process. We could not have done this without you!

We would like to thank Jan Pascoe for always being there for our family as my dad's administrative partner in ministry at National Presbyterian Church, Young Life, and as a lifelong friend who is like family to us. Our dad's "life worth living" is so much richer by God bringing you alongside him in ministry. We will never forget how you jumped in at our family's darkest time and planned our beloved brother's Celebration of Life memorial service. There is no one who has always been there for us in the little and big details of life as you have. You are a cherished, lifelong friend. This book would not have happened without you being a huge part of the team. Thank you!

We would like to thank Lee Corder for his faithful friendship and for his initiative and leadership in bringing the players together for this team of people who helped our dad to get this book written.

We would like to thank Jeff Chesemore, senior writer for Young Life and longtime friend, for using his incredible writing and editing skills and for taking the time to take everything and pull it together. You took what our dad and mom wrote, plus all of the many contributions people graciously sent in, to combine everything beautifully into this book. Thank you.

We would also like to thank Rick Theule for graciously offering to help tell our dad's story by taking time to read and help edit the final draft. Thank you also to Mike O'Leary and Tuck Knupp for reading the drafts throughout the writing process and offering their feedback as faithful friends of our dad and family throughout the years.

We would like to thank Sissi Haner for doing an amazing job proofreading this book. We appreciate your generosity and kindness in proofreading this book without even knowing us personally. You exceeded our expectations with the outstanding job you did.

We would like to thank Abebaw Eshetu for reaching out to us to help however he could to contribute to this book and for gathering letters from Ethiopian friends and getting them to us. What a joy to read all those letters! A big thank you also to Hailu Tirusew for taking the time and effort to translate all of these treasured letters.

We would like to thank David Kindred for graciously and generously offering his time and skills so that these photos could be included in the book.

For those of you who sent in contributions for this book to help fill in the gaps in our dad's memory, thank you. It was so fun to hear stories of our dad's amazing sense of humor and ways that God used our dad to impact people's lives.

And to those we may have missed thanking, please know we are grateful for you! We appreciate all the kind and gracious words that have described our dad's life and his impact.

Ultimately, we thank God for how He has loved our dad and mom so well and used their lives to reach others with the message that our dad has always shared: God loves us and, because of that, we all have *a life worth living.*

Forever thankful,

Hollie Reinhold Birckhead and Josh Reinhold for Chuck and Linda Reinhold

ABOUT THE AUTHOR

With Chuck Reinhold, everything begins and ends with Jesus.

Now seventy-nine and struggling with short-term memory issues, Chuck has spent his entire adult life in the service of his beloved Savior, primarily through the ministry of Young Life, a mission devoted to "introducing adolescents to Jesus Christ and helping them grow in their faith."

Chuck embodies the term "pioneer." From starting ministries in places like Maryland, New York, and Ethiopia, to creating a training program for the equipping of hundreds of men and women to reach kids, Chuck is a man who has lived, loved, and led well. In both Young Life and the church, he has pointed others to Jesus and spurred them on in their relationship with Him, and he's done so with self-deprecating humor and humility.

Chuck has been married to Linda, the love of his life, for over fifty years. Chuck and Linda spend their time living with their son Josh and his family in Northern Virginia, and their daughter Hollie and her family in Nashville, Tennessee.

For more information, see www.chuckreinhold.com and www.alifeworthlivingbook.com.

Morgan James
Speakers Group

We connect Morgan James published
authors with live and online events
and audiences who will benefit
from their expertise.

Morgan James makes all of our titles available
through the Library for All Charity Organization.

www.LibraryForAll.org

9 781642 791297